More critical acclaim for

RUIN AND BEAUTY

This extraordinary collection of poems is written by a woman who has spent a lifetime travelling to the center of the unconscious. Deena Metzger enters the darkest of moments and always comes back singing. She is teacher and healer, she is both guide and woman warrior.

Ruin and Beauty is an extraordinary book. Here, Metzger listens to animals, trees, rocks, oceans—she has learned their language well. She converses with other poets. She walks with sorrow and joy as companions, over deserts, through thickets, woods, and fields.

I am awestruck by what she knows. This is a prayerbook, a long letter to the gods, a secret conversation with the animal kingdom. She is trying to save us all. The passion in these poems burns holes in my mind. Metzger opens the door through which a multitude can enter. If you follow her, you will be changed by this journey, but you will learn many secrets of the universe, and perhaps you will find hope for the future as well.

—Judith Minty
Author, *Yellow Dog Journal*

Deena Metzger has spent a life in fierce devotion to the words and action that cut through to where spirit still resides in the ruins of our shattered world. Now, in *Ruin and Beauty*, Deena gifts us with poems that serve as life preservers. This is a singular vision honed over a lifetime. I can imagine seekers carrying this book five centuries from now and reciting these poems, much as we do Kabir and Rumi and Hafiz, to keep the spirit alive under daunting conditions.

—Edward Tick
Author, *War And The Soul*
Founder/Director Soldier's Heart

Ruin and Beauty

New and Selected Poems

Blessings,

Deena Metzger

🐦 RED HEN PRESS | *Los Angeles, CA*

Layout by Sydney Nichols

ISBN: 978-1-59709-425-2
Library of Congress Catalog Card Number: 2009923101

The Annenberg Foundation, the National Endowment for the Arts, the California Arts Council, and the James Irvine Foundation partially support Red Hen Press.

Published by Red Hen Press
www.redhen.org

First Edition

Acknowledgements

Author's Note: These poems are arranged according to content and resonance rather than chronology. The arrangement of a book is also a poem. The section titles have to do with the themes that I have been working for my entire life. That is why the poem that I wrote at age three, "My Plant"—the only one in chronological order—is included. From its inception it already had addressed so much I still think about.

Some of these poems have previously appeared in journals and publications over the years. However, I have never been able to keep track of them. Please accept my gratitude with apologies and without citation.

The following poems were published in: *The First Ten*, "My Plant"; *Dark Milk* (Momentum Press, 1978): "Confirmations," "Cows," and "Crimes Against Soft Birds"; *The Axis Mundi Poems* (Jazz Press, 1981): "Carry the Burning Teeth in My Two Good Breasts," "Fire Over Wood," "The Great Elm That Used to Be," "I Can See the Dead Crossed Limbs," "No Roots Are Mine," "O Love My Enemy Bite Your Bitter Root," "Out of Old Wood Long Season," "Return," "She Brings Forth Green Leaves," "Which of These Forms Have You Taken?," and "Wolf Leave Tracks Now"; *Looking for the Faces of God* (Parallax Press, 1989): "Alchemy," "Become One with Me," "Between the Worlds," "Bird Calls," "Breaking Ground," "The Buddha of the Beasts," "Burning the Night," "Canta," "Desertion," "Endarkening," "Herons, the Shadows They Cast," "I Wrote My Lover a Letter Without Words," "Icon," "Leavings," "Looking for the Faces of God," "No Words for Rumi," "Nuptuals," "Owl," "Ruminations," "Setting Out," "Silence for My Father," "Sometimes Afraid of the Ignoble End," "Sometimes in Concert with the Gods," "Song," "That Woman Is Talking to Herself," "Thorn," "The Trees Ask Me Home," "Under the Sorrow Tree," "Who Knows What the Thirst Is For," "What Shakes Me," and "Wild"; and *A Sabbath Among the Ruins* (Parallax Press, 1992): "The Bird in the Heart of the Tree," "Cambridge: Joyce," "Cape Cod: Caitlin," "The Death of the Wolf," "Defeats," "Dreaming the Road," "The Earth of Pablo Neruda," "Exploring with Neruda," "In the Morning Walking," "Invocation," "Maguey," "Moon in Taurus," "Moonshine," "Naming Us by Our Eyes," "Opening All the Doors to the Rain," "Pablo Speaks About the Girl," "Provincetown: Barbara," "Provincetown: Jane," "A Sabbath Among the Ruins," "She Laments the Death of Pablo Neruda," "Someone Remembers the Colors of Birds," "Something in the Belly," "Speaking with Neruda," "The Still Point Turning Away," "Walking with Neruda," "The Winter of Pablo Neruda," "The Work to Know What Life Is," "Threnody for Camellias," and "Valyermo: Naomi."

Table of Contents

Service at the Earth Altar

Trees Walking to Water

Singing to the Dead

Walking with Neruda

Hidden Light

Gathering at the Gates

River of Light

Ruin and Beauty

A *Note on* Ruin and Beauty

Deena Metzger's *Ruin and Beauty: New and Selected Poems* is the record of a life lived at the heart of what it means to be human when one sees living as a sacred task. I see no reason, based on the evidence of these poems and my knowledge of the poet, to believe that this vow will change. Having just closed the covers of the manuscript, I find myself feeling as I often do after one of our many long conversations over what seems lifetimes; seen, met, cared for, and confirmed by the vision and compassion of this poet who has dedicated herself and her writing to nourishing life in all its forms, and mending the rift, all rifts, in the hope of healing the world. A sacred task, indeed.

Curiously, I also find myself smiling as the words of the Japanese poet/monk Ryokan come to mind:

> Who says my poems are poems?
> My poems are not poems!
> Only when you understand this,
> Can we begin to discuss *poetry*.

Poems that are not poems, or are not *just* poems—well said in regard to Deena Metzger's poetry, for her writing sings the heart of the world with such authenticity and depth of emotion that only Lorca's *duende* suffices to name the quality of being she and her poetry have faithfully sustained over the years, word by word, line by line, to make it all come alive.

The poems in this volume reveal the development of a lifelong vision and understanding of our world as the poet finds it. From first to last, and I should say here that they have not been chronologically determined, these poems are rooted in her commitment to never take the easy road, or flinch as some might when faced with either the awesome or the terrible, no matter the circumstances in which these are engaged. In writing these words, I am reminded of the extraordinary photograph taken by her friend, Hella Hammid, and released almost three decades ago. The photograph shows Deena, a woman of some forty years, naked to the waist, with one tender breast present and the other removed due to cancer and the mastectomy she'd decided to take on to save her life. For those who have not seen the image, this courage teacher has made a gift of her body to other women, and to all, by raising her arms and joyously turning her face to the heavens so that we might see what the holy tree of life looks like when it takes a human form. But it doesn't stop there, for traveling unimpeded from her outstretched arm across the wounded flesh to her heart is the tattoo of a living branch bravely tendered, so that we might understand that life is not easily vanquished; life wants to live, and will, despite the destructive forces that besiege us at every turn.

Like her poems, this image is a testament to one of Deena Metzger's core beliefs, that when we remain open and humbly follow the voice of our native genius, creativity and compassion, we will discover ways to move forward against all odds with the sacred duties that life confers. *It is a matter of spirit*, I believe she would say.

Finally, with regard to this photograph whose content is emblematic of her poetry, when I returned to look at it as reference for these notes, I was genuinely moved to rediscover the poem Deena had written to accompany the image. As I read them, the final lines alone reveal what it looks like when one embodies her vision to live as a poet in the flesh for real:

> *I have designed my chest with the care given to an illuminated manuscript.*
> *I am no longer ashamed to make love. Love is a battle I can win.*
> *I have the body of a warrior who does not kill or wound.*
> *On the book of my body, I have permanently inscribed a tree.*

"Born young into a world already old," poet Louis Zukofsky wrote, to explain our contemporary human dilemma. It is a formulation that can lay claim to a wisdom of its own; but, it is not enough, as the poems herein make clear. They are rooted in a spirit source that leaves no room for turning away from the considerable burden history places upon each person and new generation, despite the compelling nature of one's justification or view. Deena knows that no one is innocent in a terrible time; that each of us has been given a voice and that each voice given comes with a demand. It is a demand she embraces. And so her poetry shows us how we may engage the encumbrance and obligation of history by providing us with a visionary path that can transform our troubling inheritance into a new ground on which, together, we may stand.

Ruin and Beauty, well named, provides a map, then, a pathway through, to help us navigate life's uncertain and always shifting topography, though she is wily as all lovers are, for it is not an easy thing to accomplish. Sometimes, the path is indicated subtly with a line that seems to wink as one fellow traveler might wink to another, *enter here*, or the path appears as a phrase that rises out of the body of the poem suddenly with an articulate beauty that changes how a reader sees. (I don't know with accuracy how her poetry manages this, but even while leading a reader far from the safety of previous perceptions and beliefs, there is something—a voice—that reassures readers as they confront their long held views.) At other times she brings to bear the ferocious commitment of a revolutionary who knows that in this dimming world the stakes are life itself, and so she challenges all of our assumptions, defenses, and justifications head on, while always maintaining a heart that reminds us when life's rigor has worn us to the bone, *There is no moment that is not for loving.*

These are elements of the multifaceted nature and orientation of her poetics. I don't think I stretch too far to say that the effect of the principles underlying her poetry is reminiscent of the sword carried by Manjusri, the Buddhist bodhisattva of wisdom. Where needed, one edge of the blade is life giving, while the other hones in on personal and collective delusions that bring harm to our world, and aims to take them away. Metzger wields her poetic sword, as it were, with the utmost care, for in addition to her vow to do no harm she recognizes that the promise of language is not only to mirror the world, but to help create it. This is the life-giving aspect of her poetry. Her commitment to such creation places her poetry in alliance with the twentieth century Spanish poet, Juan Ramón Jimenez, who understood the transformative power of language, and longed for "*the exact name of things / that my word may be / the thing itself / recreated by my soul.*"

But why does he want that? Why does she? What is the use of a poetry that seeks to transform words into the real? The response Jimenez provides in his poem, "Mind, Give Me," reveals a part of the quest these poets share, one that Deena knows like the pattern of her own breathing:

> *So that all who do not know them*
> *go through me,*
> > *to things.*
> *All who have forgotten*
> *go through me,*
> > *to things.*
> *All those who love them*
> *go through me,*
> > *to things. . . .*

Poet as conduit, poet as source. Or, as Yeats would have it, poet as priest. It is a spiritual understanding of the power of naming that calls to mind both western and eastern roots. In the former, as we have been told from our earliest days, the light that lit up the universe in the beginning was created at the source by the saying of its name. This is the west's primary model of the power of a creator—in whose image we are told we are made—to name things into the world. It is also a pragmatic and compassionate view that knows the imagination is without boundary; what it proposes *is* possible when we live rooted in its boundless provenance.

But, Deena also holds that naming is more a matter of primary and radical *listening* than of speech. In this she exemplifies the Vedic teachings that tell us that at some point in time each thing made the sound of its essential nature or soul; tree, for example, made the sound of the essence of tree, river and stone did the same, as did sky and mountain, serpent and bear, so that when humans first heard these sounds they took them up naturally as the name for each thing, for they experienced the world as sentient, magical, and imbued with spirit, which is precisely what Deena's poetry reveals.

To dedicate one's passion for the sentient and beautiful of our world, while maintaining the courage and love to attempt a transformation of all that would destroy it, is the life of this poet. Poem after poem makes clear her conviction that the purity of being found in the beginning, "*when all beings partook / and drank of beauty / as if it were pure water*" still remains, despite the ruin our species has rained down against it.

As such, her poetry not only acknowledges primal beauty as the nature of life itself, it seeks to rekindle it through the power to name.

As an experimental and somewhat mischievous act of divination to honor the spirit of this collection and the poet who wrote these poems, (over the years, Deena's coyote spirit has led her to devise many ways of her own to divine), I leafed through the manuscript and selected lines at random three times to see if what I've been saying is really true. All poets, I believe, should be willing to face a test of this order. I also did so with a great seriousness to see if the language alone would lead me to its source, the place of silence where *"voices we do not understand / become transparent,"* the place before any word is spoken, where a poet sometimes merges entirely with her world. As she writes:

> *If I can disappear myself,*
> *I may also,*
> *as I know myself, disappear,*
> *the way wind disappears,*
> *in order finally to know, in this life*
> *something of what is.*

Here is what I found:

> *I think I must be the tree*
> *but also the hole in it*
> *pecked out by a sharp beak*

And:

I am saying the name of my friend. I am saying it again and again. I am saying it like a rosary or a cord of amber beads, or a mantra of jade, or the fringe on a tallit, or a necklace of turquoise and silver, or a prayer wheel loose in the wind. I am turning the hour and the day and the year on the axis of his name. I am watching the earth spin on the point of the sacred alphabet of his name. I am spinning the bombs away. I am spinning them faster than light. I am spinning the silver of bombs into a thread of light that cannot disappear us. As long as I remember my friend, he will stay alive.

And, finally:

> *give me everything mangled and bruised,*
> *and I will make a light of it to make you weep,*
> *and we will have rain,*
> *and begin again.*

This is the poet's vision, then, in her own words. It is part of her intent. It arcs from the heart of what she is, and what she has made in her more than seventy years, to the heart of the world and back again. It is a möbius strip, a DNA channel of mutual creation that moves her to her writing desk so that she may, with grace, discover its shape in a language of offering. But, why? Always the question precedes, and always the answer is partial: So that we, too, may hold beauty, have vision and understand. For when we do, we enter into the conversation poetry is, and sometimes discover our own pathway through to the poem already alive within us, the poem of this very moment, waiting to be found.

—Peter Levitt
Salt Spring Island, British Columbia

from *The First Ten*

My Plant

It does not grow in water,
It does not grow in dirt or sand,
But in happy children's hands.[1]

---

1 Spoken, 1939. from *The First Ten*, 1946.

Bright Omens

Augury

Suddenly the sky rains gulls.
Pelicans, pigeons, crows, ravens,
hawks dart through our hands
in patterns of flight and wind,
the silver threads of elsewhere in their beaks.
This is the weaving of invisible,
shimmering worlds
into a single fabric of mind.
We call this the
augury of the birds.

The Great Elm That Used to Be[2]

She told me about divining,
called it witching,
returning the water rights.
You take a forked branch,
the water calls it,
if it is dead
how does the tree hear the call?
Where we walk was once sky
and falling,
angels hurled down,
gathering in deep dark pools.
Ask, then,
about the underworld,
the hidden springs,
the trees of breath.

---

2   Title from "Once and Again" by Hayden Carruth, in *Brothers I Love You All.*

Fire Over Wood

As long as there is wood below, the fire burns above[3]

It is four o'clock and dark. Where the bough
hovers is the nest of the night bird.
I learn to read shadows. Fortune is the dark patch
when moving. Winter solstice approaches,
snow as the only light.

Words tame us, domestic crumbs in the woods
for the furry guest. By the light of my window
I am unable to name what prowls on delicate clawed feet.
These images protect me against the early dark.
I am not ready enough for what I love.
I am neither hunter nor hunted. The truth:
in the forest, I have been known to stand aside.

The I Ching offered stillness, but I drew fire.
This morning I saw the leaves burning
in the lake. Fire relies on our breath.
I stop breathing. Animals of the night
are predatory and have great yellow eyes.
The dark is independent of every one of us.

---

3   The I Ching – Hexagram 50 Ting

O Love My Enemy Bite Your Bitter Root[4]

It is Sunday, a great wind wraps
about the trees. The pine explodes wild skunk
scent in the shaking air. What comes
fresh has already traveled the night
through the lives we love. Everything
must have a home. Winter is closer than
we think, let it come fast and unsparingly,
O! not the bitter but the sharp. Something
waits in the woods invisible in the wind,
shape of the angel wrestling me finally
to the stone ground.

Now, I sit with the tree asking the dryad
to live a long time.

---

4   Title from "Gacela of the Bitter Root" by Federico Garcia Lorca, in *Dream & Other Writings*, new versions by Edwin Honig.

Gacela of Deer and Shovel

He was digging the grave.
No, he was digging a womb
of earth where the pepper tree
would be planted in her memory.
That is, the tree would be in the soil of memory.
Isn't that what the phrase means?

He looked up, the man said,
his back to the grave where a wolf was buried,
while to the east, another pepper tree,
this one of birth,
was flourishing after sixteen years,
and the girl, in whose future it had been planted,
now also red berried, tongued and nippled,
and her fine, narrow leaves, long dark tresses,
meeting the wind,
in its original rhythms, its ragas and movements.

He looked up, the ex-soldier said,
and saw the deer, four of them,
the doe, gacela, her two fawns
and the buck with his great rack.
They paused, as they do, one
leg bent up, the hoof pointed down,
alert, but not yet in the grace
of movement, until the living wolf
pranced toward.

You can say, it was hunter
and hunted, predator and prey,
but I think it was the swift dance
they learn on the other side
of light, and come here to enact.

The shovel, sharp then in the earth,
again and again.
The young pepper tree
waiting to be planted.
Death and birth
giving us the Gacela and the Shovel.
She, in whose memory

we were planting the pepper,
called her own land, Ruach,
wind and breath and spirit,
which is not a contradiction
as earth and air intermingle
like gacela and wolf,
or earth and shovel.

He was digging into the earth,
after years in Iraq,
taken by the rhythm of the shovel,
but looked up in time
to see the gacela, the two fawn,
the buck with a huge rack
and the young wolf mother
running with them
in the cycle of leaping
and descending.

He was digging into the earth
with a shovel, and looked up
to see the gacela, the two fawn
and the buck with a huge rack.
Behind him a grave
where another wolf lay buried,
and the young wolf mother
speeding toward the deer
past the pepper tree of the daughter,
past the small olive tree in the south,
the place where I will be buried
in the womb of earth.

Between the Worlds

Flesh like metal,
spirit like mist,

teach me the gait
of the luminous wolves
drinking
from the dark river.

In those waters
the stones sing.

Can the world
mend
in this body?

Sometimes Afraid of the Ignoble End

Bees in the last honey of the dead hummingbird,
have mercy on us.
Was it always so,
these small, frequent deaths?
I gather the amputated wings,
the deserted nests
and make an altar.
May my dead be with me!
May the candles flutter!
The sky is red and gray
with the rain of feathers,

May there be sweetness
to the last.

No Words for Rumi

Silence pours into me
as a cataract of wine
overflowing the sides
of a glass chasm.
If I do not speak
I will die.
If I do speak,
this silence
that has become my breath
will disappear.
How can I pretend
these are not words
or how can I speak
when I am drinking
and under water?

The order of things,
the wine flooding
down the mountain,
is so sweet,
I fear
there is no end to it.

Calling the Wind

I called the wind and it came. Or the wind called me and I responded. History shattered then and tradition reconstituted itself. A conversation that had fallen into silence re-established, stuttering here, faltering there, unsure but blooming in sudden epiphanies of rain or the assent of branches describing miniscule galactic arcs, ellipses of movement and light.

I came to a bare plain, swept clear of all impediments first by the unceasing purity of snow, then by hungry fires speeding from range to range. Here where no things are seen, the words finally uttered fell like seeds from supernovas casting the world anew. The sun spoke paragraphs of light and the rain drowned us in prophecy.

In this we're not alone. In errant gusts prickly pines, stiff handed cypresses, firs and redwoods bend and tremble as the intelligence of all things leans toward divine intent.

At the base of an olive tree, under the September sun, I offered myself up. It was almost all there: earth, air, fire. Then another wind, blue, wet and cool, arose, inserting itself between pressed palms of desert heat. Salted where the other wind had carried sage. It settled the yellow dust and briefly wrapped itself about my hands and face. Longing for the presence of the sea, I fell into the language of all things.

That's how it was. I thought I called the wind and that it came, but what had happened was the wind called me and I went. Brokenness or despair bringing me back to elementals, thinking of power but wanting prayer and placing one letter against another the way a knowing child piles up stones. Not wanting ever again to be outside the world and so opening the door of water in the air.

Bread Offerings

Making bread offerings
to the gulls,
God's hungry angels,
week after week,
became a way
of calling the invisible
into a feather
that afterwards could heal
even the broken wing
that happened to be
my own.

A gull took the crumbs
at the sacred island
and walked along the wall,
so close we held our breath;
then a male landed,
Annunciation,
in a flurry of raised wings.
We gathered stubborn faith
from this sign and from the pelicans
flying around and around
the cliffs in a corona of light.

The simple repetition
of an activity,
the old woman feeding
pigeons in the city park,
or the old man on the boardwalk
emptying his lunch bag
for the most ordinary creatures,
rats and random birds,
becomes a prayer tie,
one and then another,
leafing a tree that reaches
what we cannot see.

A heidi ho
a yáha yáha yáha yáha yáha
Áhoo áhoo áhoo áhoo áhoooooo

The songs of gulls,
shrieks and sibilant vowels
and watery consonants,
and the pauses in between
where the waves break,
the triuned letters on the sand
and the eddies in the air
  calling,
    calling,
      calling out in prayer.

Expecting to Get Snowed In

This snowfall is bitter,
an avenging cold
that is more gray than white.
We gather into the small places
we have made against adversity
and build fires to warm ourselves.
Beauty so quickly becomes sleet.
The mood turns as quickly as the weather.
Fear does it, or danger.

One believes oneself to be a small creature
with only fur or feathers
against a relentless wind
from the top of the mountain
where the gods live secretly
and visit their exile upon us.

We could not survive without our wits,
but here a small flock of birds scatters
up into the trees. It is not clear
whether their flight is desperate
or an explosion of joy.
Before the snow, they had disappeared,
were seeking water elsewhere,
now this blizzard calls them home.
This advent of their jubilation.

Gulls

A slight movement toward the hard crusts
we have gathered in a paper bag
incites the gulls from the four directions.
The empty sky floods with wings
as they land and take off again,
land and take off again.
These hungry ones fly toward us
in an explosion of beauty
not unlike dawn rupturing the dark
or sunset smearing its violet golden light.
Across the advent of night,
their beaks are crimson with their desire
for the small offerings we bring
to provoke their dance.
But we never bring
enough simple bread with us
to satisfy our craving
for their presence,
for the birds reaching toward the hands
we extend to them,
tireless in motion and motionless
as they hover in the air
just by our fingertips.
            That we should be met this way,
            that our appetite
            should be rewarded
            by such grace:
                        the utter glory of it.

Pelican Island

Pelican Island exists in the mind.
No one has ever traveled there
except the dead who soar invisibly
along the transparent currents
that ring the white cliffs.
What can I speak of here
without revealing
whether I am one of the dead?

How do I come by this knowing?
Spying and stealing. Plagiarizing.
Repeating old texts, myths and legends,
even though Pelican Island
is invulnerable
to my assault and your curiosity.
This is not another idyll
devoted to the forbidden.

You cannot go to Pelican Island.
I cannot go to Pelican Island.
Nothing will change this.
The dead have escaped us,
and the birds, recognizing
a sanctuary, circle and circle
    in endless joy.

Thirteen Dark Moons

Thirteen ring-necked pigeons appear,
each one a dark moon,
so visible in daylight,
with a band of moonstone
around its neck
and a flurry of light
hidden in the underside
of a fan of tail feathers
that opens in flight,
and when landing:
such grace.

They gather this morning
as soon as the seeds are offered,
then they return to the trees
to sing the song
their ancestors taught them
in the beginning,
when all beings partook
and drank of beauty
as if it were pure water.

Under the Sorrow Tree

By the river,
under the sorrow tree,
the universe says
the bones must dance,
and she, who goes out with a net
to catch the spirits,
returns, her hands filled
only with the dark briars
we have hummed
these many years.
The one who sees sorrow
cannot staunch it,
yet by her side
something white
announces itself.
The bones are sucked clean,
the one nearest the heart
becomes a flute,
when you blow,
the dead come
and behind them,
the other bones in a circle.

The universe says
loss demands birth
and the two
are lovers.

The Midnight Sun [Song]

Have I seen the Midnight Sun?
Sky turns black
as the light is born.

Comes the blue
that lies between
what is seen
and what's unseen.

Have I seen the Northern Lights?
Letters of flame
sign the Holy Name.

Comes the blue
that lies between
dark and light
and day and night.

Comes the green
that's in-between
what is living,
what's a dream.

Have I seen the Midnight Sun?
Birds ecstatic in the dawn.
Praise the light from Paradise,
Sky of Fire,
Sky of Ice.

Have I seen the Midnight Sun?
Rain falling on platinum.
Rainbow as a covenant,
God exists
and Beauty has won.

God exists
and Beauty has won.

The Dark Animal Gods

Icon

This
wooden
icon
is the face
of
god,
a knife
in a human hand
found it.
I am waiting
for it to speak.
If
there is a sign,
it is
　　　howl of wolf,

　　　wet muzzle,

　　　gleaming teeth.

Wild

That night cry
of a woman in the hills
is only a cougar.
The shadow
in the heart of the meadow
is the bobcat, awake.
That slouch of fur amidst
the stammering of trees
is the wild
coming down
to my palm, at last.

Moon in Taurus

Across the barbed wire, the bull takes my hand. It is lost in his mouth, deeper, softer, warmer than I dare think. This is what it must be to sink into a large woman, to submit to her ample thighs. I am aware of boundaries, his teeth, used to grass, will not close on me, he wants the salt, wants me to sweat for him.

I have had to come east to learn this animal, a real not mythic beast, attended by dozens of heifers, who seeks me out under the horned, full moon. My hands, stained with mulberries, come clean on that great tongue slapping between my fingers, his tail flits across his back, his silken tassel quivers.

I have dreamed this animal but not his gentleness, not that I would herd with him, not that I would wish him to nudge my flanks, his skin slouched over bones, a tent of a beast, not that he would drive me forward

> head down,
> > hungry,
> > > through
> > > > the night fields.

Burning the Night

Lightning tears the heart the way the air is seared, then sealed, when the Gods descend. Did you think The Presence would fail to leave a scar?

The tree, joyous with the instant of being set alight, is a great torch. Everyone knowing the chosen one by the roar of living gold, by the plume of smoke, bends toward it. Sometimes an entire forest taken down. Trees humbled but grateful for the holy flame.

Come then to the ones who endure, and ask wisdom from the charred cunt, from the dark burned cave at the root, where the Gods forged their knowledge. This, they said, is the lovemaking: "Beware."

So we go to each other hoping to die but also afraid.

That is,
    hoping to burn
That is,
    hoping to hold the fire.

To be the lightning rod of air, to blaze first with the invisible platinum stamens of stars, then to be a doorway, afterwards and for all time, through which the fierce hunger for the body enters the nest of emptiness which has become ourselves.

Is this what you want?

Cows

After the seven lean years
we are promised seven fat ones,
if the cows do not die first.
Some care must be taken
to prevent their demise
in the scrub
or the slaughterhouse.
There must be enough bones
to throw and to bury.

The skull of a cow,
I put it on.
There are many strewn in the field,
there has not been much rain.
I look through the eyes,
that is, my eyes replace the eyes
that death has taken.
I can see out or through.
It is not a bad fate
to be a cow,
to be, at once,
so awkward,
so full of grace,
so full of milk.

Everywhere the udders are full,
the teats are ready,
the mouth of the calf is soft and deep.
I would thrust my hand in it
for the wet joy of being so used.

My own breasts are marked
from the time the milk came in too fast;

I did not have time to grow
to the moment of giving.
It is fitting
that beauty
leaves such scars.

Milk has passed through my fingers,
has spurted through my fingers,
but not once
during these seven lean years.

Breaking Ground

Toward the south, through the center
of a still brown patch of weeds,
a living green line,
like marble dividing stone,
cuts the hill, a caesarean section
from navel to pubic bone.
Scar on the belly of my mother
where I tore her open.
Across the canyon, a rock face
has been split into labia
and there are hundreds of buttocks and hips,
breasts cut with a water knife
from the body rock.
Here is the winter knot
before it's cut into spring.
In my belly,
the stone of light
split open,
something green emerged
and exploded into a thousand arms.
The grass has come again,
insidious spring over the disguised rock,
the mustard returns and the lupine bruise
in the raw, scabrous wind,
now acacia, bees, moths, ants, birds
ground out of uterine stone.
This is the order:
green, earth, stone, sulphur, bedrock, fire.

    Peace and trembling
    throughout the body of the Mother.

Carry the Burning Teeth in My Two Good Breasts[5]

The wolf suckled my young
in return for promises
this breast eaten   the
cubs hungry   wind avalanches
across the plain   the nipple
hounded   is it snow
or claw   the alarm of scent
my sweet skin   the pack
condenses into a single
mouth   this milk   the
prairie teeth   hungry
my son sits in the rain
water   down his pelt
the animal oil   the stink
of hide   I hear
the she-wolf   restless
her yellow eyes ready   she
knows how to prowl   this
neighborhood will not hold
her   the first time only rabbits
the mother red faced
biting her tail   my son
we inch around the
genitals   pretending
canine   she sleeps
at the foot of the bed
he slides down the
mountain   knees up
fur on the blanket   she
is wolf   3/4s   the sharp
teeth   only one breast
remaining   she has eight teats
the howl in the evening
the moon appearing   fires
lust   my sons among the
leaves   the bedstones
are cavernous   white
teats dripping
milk out of the bitch
the man is always

---

5   Title from "Staring at the American Buffalo" by Holly Prado.

thirsty   Loba   we call her
teeth marks everywhere
pillows like chickens   the
feathers warnings   The issue
is   territory. The question is:
whose sons? Mine? Or Hers?

Afternoon

Retreat in the afternoon, dreams feathering the back of the wild goose or the swan coming down, an insistent visitation in clouds and thunder.

Who wouldn't fall on her knees, deaf to ordinary day, to the footsteps in dust, the egg woman entering, who would listen for the car when she is lost in wings and chariots, the beak rising, talons clamped on her nipples, trying to learn the bird calls?

Once, the shock of two black swans, emerging from the water, twisting, one about the neck of the other, pink billed and trumpeting, then drowning again; two rhinoceroses, heaving, one great stone wheel rubbing for a millennium against the other, also the lion, opening the burning air of the great savannah with his tawny rod.

Alone, the woman locks the door against all blind witnesses to the churning air, the down feathers, the white squawks. She hunkers down in stealthy prayer, praising the hand of god, the secret union in the stealth of afternoon.

Do Poems Have Gender or Sex?

OK. There are poems that both men and women write, and then there are poems that come only from a woman. Also, of course, poems that could only come from a man. Are the poems of a woman as good? The one of the years of needles? The poem of the desperate thread? I am thinking of needles and bayonets. Of how we are entered fine or hard. So I am wondering, what kind of poem goes to church with a gun in its pocket? I am thinking that a poem is a law. The alms lady sits outside the door. On Friday, the god puts on his woman's dress, paints his lips with rouge and comes to the *shabbas* bed. Oh god, hermes aphrodite! Oh lord, transvestite god. And with white skirts, she comes. The domes of the synagogue are blue breasts. The nipples are stars.

The woman is such a small thing in a poem. She's the little spring flower you notice as you go to war. You say, "White narcissus, it's you I'm coming home to, oh dear god." But your road is far away and brick. The woman's poem sits in a basket of bobbins and bread. Her shoulders are narrow, a river could divide them. But the man is strong. Give him a lever and his poem lifts the moon from its orbit. She's only the comet, a flash of light. And the Lord? "Lord, lord. Lord, lord."

I read Amachi and his voice comes right into my poem. "Just like a man," I say, "he can't stay out of any hole." He's like the poem of the *kuchlefl*, wanting to stir everyone's pot. I am thinking maybe it's I.B. Singer who's entered. And why not? They are both lusty men whose words, cocksmen and drunkards, crow at every corner as if the air were free. A woman is such a small street and hobbled with cobblestones. The man's poem is a cart with four horses. I nearly wrote corpses. He knocks at the door and asks for a room. "Is there something to eat?" Embroidered linen unfolding under his head.

It's *shabbas* and the man must come home. When She comes from the sky, the rooster gathers his hens for the prayers of the egg. It's Sunday, the marble is cold. On Monday, the road again, bricks and blood. On Tuesday, the blood stained sheets on the line. On Wednesday, the quarry dust, the flax. On Thursday, God says, "This is a poem, this hewn stone, this scaffold, this up and down." On Friday, She turns up her hem. You cannot see a stitch. The little needles go in and out, so fine, so fine.

Succubus

It's in the mouth. From *suc*, to go, from *cumbre*,
cubare, to lie down. To go. To lie down.

From *succu*, juice from, *succu* juices, from *lentus*,
full of. It is in the mouth, full of juices.
We go. We lie down. The demon, the evil one,
she comes in our sleep, they say.
He says, she is a strumpet. She sucks out our juices.
We have been going, we have been going to lie down.
We did not expect her.

We thought we could keep the juices, but
the apricot falls fleshly to the ground
and the soil sucks it in, peaches. And then
sweet under our feet, rises up, tree sap,
maple syrup and the earth opens her mouth.
Gives it back. Sun sucking it up.
It's the white juice, the milkweed in my mouth,
the seed pod liquid and opening about safe teeth.
Teeth planted in the earth. From the dragon.
Snake woman. Her tail in her own mouth. Sucking.
I take what I can, sucking my own fingers.
As a child, thumb in the mouth. He can't suck
his own cock. The milk wants to exit,
little seeds we can't see with the eye.
An entire army from teeth. Teeth seeds,
white and ivory. The army turns
against the dragon. She lies down. Dying,
it is called. Fear of the snake. She
is healing. Climbs up the rod toward the sun.
The snake of Dionysus. Then Apollo stole it.
They link. The sun. Soil. Plowing.
Dark furrows opening and spreading wide to the hoe.
In earthquake seasons, earth heaves up. Hips
dark and hungry. Little white seeds buried deep.

Did he ever commit sodomy? Did he find a goat or
mare inviting? Did he ever? Fellatio? From *felare*,
to suck. Did he ever? Did she ever? Succubus.
Juices. Comes in the night. Didn't he lie down?
Did he go, didn't he go, didn't he go to lie down?
Wasn't it an invitation?

So succulent, so full of juices, so
full of, so full of us. Succubus. Lie down.
Juices. So full of, so full, O so full, us
sucking. O so full. Sucking. These juices.
Succu. Lent means spring.

Owl

For my birthday, you give me the wing of a dead owl to lie beside the wing of another. My Cherokee friend said, "Owl can be dangerous. It can cause the air to turn black as the path of Owl streaking toward a mouse. It can cast spells for years after its death." Native peoples agree, "Owl is strong medicine."

I tried to teach the black cat, Hecate, what no mother cat had taught her, shook her in the air when the mating owls hooted; it was not sufficient. She disappeared on Halloween, the night after I'd held her in my arms, looking in her yellow eyes, saying, "We are strange companions."

Hecate, like Lilith, is the owl goddess, the goddess of crossroads, of caves and dark places. The gods in all their forms take themselves back, again and again, into themselves.

You found the wing on the road among other wings. On my altar, I put what a man had mutilated. I take a chance. Trust is one of the trials of the dharma.

On your birthday, Owl is sentinel over the darkening meadow. You spy its silhouette against the sky, a practice developed as a child. We sit on stones staring in different directions. This small circle might also mark the rise of the sun or moon.

In our calendars, this is the end of the first year we have known each other. We have been given the task of loving with every conscious breath.

It does not matter that the owl does not answer our calls when we hoot to it. The who of the female is lower than the who of the male. They hoot and echo, hoot and echo. After six months, the wing you gave me is living in the meadow.

Heat

Sometimes
under the blindfold of night,
my phantom lover leads me naked
to the mud banks
of subterranean rivers,
raven at my breast
and the dark song
of trees moist between my thighs.
There we make hands
from the underbrush of desire,
calling the glowing arrow
of the first summer storm
to descend on us like estrus.
We breathe the scent of it,
I fall to my knees
like all the creatures I love
until he howls,
and the golden eyes of wolves,
mountain lions and stags,
light the rest of our way down.

Maguey

Like the zen master,
you came with the sword.

The gentle woman who taught me, said
"The rose *and* the thorn."
You want to catch in my flesh.

I watch the century plant
shoot a green staff into the air.

I tell you how the stamens hook
out of the stalk, they will . . .

"Flower," you say,
wanting the yellow rain,

pulque, mescal, tequila
out of the green spiny leaves.

Walking to the olive tree,
thistles catch in my clothes,
burrs in my hands and feet,

everything asking to be carried.
Why do you weep in rage,
when I cry out?

Even the Buddha wolf knows the spike,
carries seeds from one place to another;
they grasp at him.

The crown of thorns:
the life holding on.

The Huichols say, "In this life
no one goes lacking
for something with which to get stuck in the eye."

In the desert
we become tenacious.

How did we say it when I was a kid?
"I'm hooked."

The day you visit:
Maguey—a green maypole
out of a rosette of razors

speeds past my window—
twelve feet in a week
—to dissolve in sperm milk of yellow flowers.

Still, we cannot pretend
it is easy.

Honey for Oshun at My Wedding

Knowing that honey
is the disguise fire uses
to enter into the embrace of water,
as yellow jets of sulfur from the center
of the earth are water's way
to endure in fire, I take
from the hive at my core
and give it as a gift
to the one who takes us
into the entire river
of her being.
As you look on,
I offer myself
absolutely
and we descend
so sweetly
in the rills, the eddies
and the tides.

Raspberries

We passed the raspberries between us, after you carried them a half mile—swimming in your mouth. They were intact, the taste of you inhabited the dark center. You came out of the river, a goat boy, dripping, hair curled into god's horns.

Kiwis cut into the perfect lunar circle of cunt, all the long slices of white fruit, the silk of corn, the daring fuzz of apricot, the hard grind of cherry stones. Fruit washed in the river glistens before the knife creates the longing of one half for another.

We were devoured under the dark waters, taken up into the roots, exploded into the air in bristling yellow pollen of pine, only a bit of us remaining in the tang and bite of fruit in the musk and blood of berries, in the sting.

Our smallest fingers fit in the red pulp, it spread open, calling back the stem. We carried the river in our hair, every atom of our bodies had once been the others. Wherever we touched there were entrances, filled with raspberries.

I Wrote My Lover a Letter Without Words

I said,
I am a small woman,
bold enough to want
to hold a planet in my broken heart.

I said,
Here stillness falls
upon the shoulder of stillness,
as one shadow disappears in another.
Everything is here
in the point of this moment of air.

I said,
Under this hand of silence,
this woman comes to life,
like a waterfall undressing itself.

I said,
Reduced to a needle of light,
I am completely myself.

I said,
In each moment,
the story of the universe is repeated:
There was nothing.
     Look what is coming to be.
     You always surprise me.

Watching Michael Roar

I

You run fast,
your great horns
bruise the adamant bark,
sparks fly through the trees,
the stones catch fire
and the rain
which extinguishes all,
descends through fists
of white ecstatic light.

II

This fire
has nothing to burn
until we're broken
and offer
these shards to lick.
Fire has a mouth
which is unequalled.

III

Grief, my love,
then shattering,
then the heart,
crawling like a living thing,
hungry and naked.

IV

The exultant stretch
of your neck,
your transparent mouth
open and singing,
your body
trembling in the void.
The silence
of the gods descending
into our two bodies.

V
Cornea of stars,
chest of helium,
great stellar nitrogen shriek
of song,
you reach up,
lightning rod,
and pull everything down.

VI
You wanted ashes?
Here is the hoof print
of god upon your temple
and some embers, burning
like thorns,
in my mouth.

VII
Feathers singed,
my little angel,
your wings dark
with fire,
the brand of your lips
on my breastbone.
When you cried out,
I saw the flame,
soot falling
onto my eyes.

VIII
Angel,
light of your wings,
burns.
Fire
is easier, it
can be put out.

IX

I've seen you ride
this two-headed beast,
four legs to make
one body, flank
galloping on flank,
trembling and rearing,
the rider
thrown
into the stars.

What Feeds Us

I imagine your sperm in my mouth
swift as salmon jumping the rapids,
cool as phosphorescent fish spawning
in the night waters,
urgent as the rut of sheep
in the snow fields
of the Himalayas
or the primordial pumping of lava
up from the molten core
through a newborn grassy cone of earth
breaking into a torrential rain,
the sparks still flying
as the living milk runs
out of your body
to the estuaries
of my desire,
    and I drink.

Hungry Every Morning

The peach tree is content. Each year a limb breaks and
the ground rots with mashed fruit. Nothing to eat
but the weight of it. I want the hunger, the goose cry
of the body streaking North North.

Where's the lusty woman I knew? Even her wine tamed.
Sipping delicate liebfrau, lunch on glass plates,
remembers the squawk of those waterfowl, cunt and cock.

This flesh is tired of its shape. The atoms of my skin
beg to shine with the color red. I want his body.
I am tired of living in the world.

Solitary from the woods, I arrange cattails
in a friend's vase. Fine white hairs breaking
from the bulging reed. Who said spring's a maiden?

Before my eyes, the bougainvillea with thorny speed
leaps magenta toward the white magnolia bulb.
This morning the dandelions feather sperm
through the conjugal air.

Hawk lady, I want my prey.
   Break me in the dive,
      in the ravenous mouth.

When You Marry a Young Man

The sun rises in the middle of the night, then
something you've forgotten awakens you,
you give up dreaming
for what is restless beside you on the pillow.
You remember need, the urgencies of flesh;
sleep, food, grief, exultation
become the lights around the nebula of your dying,
the fire of him, the shadow of his light at your outer edges
falls back upon your dark center.

His appearance in winter,
like a cardinal pecking at the snow
or the snow itself illuminating night,
or a jay, blue, against the silver of the rain,
or the light of the rain against the darkness.
is not an eclipse, but the star steady in its burning
in the night *and* the day
    these visitations,
        hallucinations,
            desires.

Vows [Song]

Where you branch in me,
I do not know,
nor which leaves
are my mouth,
nor why your roots
are my fingers,
yet I will travel you
though you be unmoving,
into the dark earth
and into the sky.

Where you rise in me,
I do not know,
nor why your light
is my hair,
nor why your shadows
are songs,
yet, I will travel you
though you be flying,
into the white dawn
and into the night.

The Work to Know What Life Is

At night, when you were in my body, when you were the tree giving breath to the night, I took it in. We lay there, your mouth open against mine with the breath going back and forth. I said, "This is the Amazon. I want to grow dark as a jungle with you, to feed all the myriad birds, to give off air to breathe." We lay together, dark woods feeding the universe, you breathing into me, I, taking your breath, holding it in my body, saying "Life, Life, Life."

I wanted to be a plant form. I wanted to laugh under you like grass, to bend and ripple, to be the crisp smell, to be so common about you, to be everywhere about you, to house the small, and be there under your body when you rolled there, where I was.

I wanted to be the animal form. I wanted to howl, to speak the moon language, to rut with you as the August moon tipped toward roundness and the blood poured out of my body. I held your penis that had plunged into me, and afterwards my hands were red with my own blood. I wanted to paint our faces, to darken our mouths, to make the mark of blood across our bodies, to write "Life, Life, Life" in the goat smell of your hands. You carried it all day on your fingers, as I carried your pulse in my swollen cunt, the beat repeating itself like a heart. My body had shaped itself to yours, was opening and closing.

I wanted to be the forms of light, to be the wind, the vision, to burn you like a star, to wrap you in a storm, to make the tree yield. I wanted to drown in your white water, and where your fingers probed I wanted to hear each pore cry out, "Open, Open. Break Open! Let nothing be hidden or closed."

I wanted to be all the violent openings, all earthquake and avalanche, and the quiet, all the dawns and dusks, all the deep blues of my body, the closing and opening of light. I wanted to be the breath from the lungs of the universe, and to open your mouth with a tongue of rain, to touch all the corners and joinings. When you entered me, when I heard you cry, "Love me, love me, love me with your mouth," I wanted to take you in with everything wet and fiery, to enter you with breath until you also called out and called out and called, "Life, Life, Life."

Ruminations

For Michael
by Deena

For Deena
by Michael Ortiz Hill

After months of planning
I finally met you
by accident.

Now that we love each other
I am afraid.
When I conjured love,
I had no fear.
As before God,
I dedicate myself,
but afterwards,
in The Presence,
I am afraid.

The night before we met
I dreamt you were a giantess
with two singing daughters.
Next morning, I found
you would fit well under my arm
[the proverbial dove]
that your voice was from Brooklyn
and very soft.

There is nowhere to go after this,
I am accustomed to running forward or away.
This morning,
in the midst of a dry summer,
it rained.

I said, "In my heart of hearts
I want to know you as a lover."
You didn't answer.
I could have died in your silence.
I said, "I am not carrying
a concealed blade."
And for a second you held belief and disbelief
in a wry smile.

When you touch me,
I cannot tell

if you are taking something
or making an offering.

Then the Buddhists came
and planted a small monument for peace
right in the middle of our conversation.
The little Japanese girl refused to nibble
the wild fennel
I had picked for her.

Bright orange phallus parting
the labia of a mussel
in the Italian restaurant;
the century plant blooms
once every hundred years.
If it's not one thing
it's another.

No matter who else you meet
in this world
even after I die,
I am the one.
This is what is so surprising:
we planned this,
only the bodies and lives
have been given to us.
Now we must undress,
it is more fearful since
it isn't the first time,
and it is.
I've done this so many times with you,
that is why I'm always forgetting.

I never met someone
I more enjoy giving gifts to.
I've always wanted to love you well.
This is the dharma I cannot betray.

Because I belong to you,
I know you can never leave me,
if there isn't this life,

there's the next one,
and there's always
the first one
that neither of us
can leave.

The first summer I loved you,
I could not stop touching
the absence of your breast.
This pale body loved your dark skin,
this young boy liked to trace his fingers
along the wrinkles near your eyes.

Last night in your sleep,
despite our vow of silence,
you spoke to me
of mundane matters,
like your love for me.

Under arrest in Honduras
the frightened boy with his gun
slung over his shoulder
shouting at me,
I reminded myself
"Just one more border to cross
and I will be in the arms of my lover."
I get a little crazy,
I never could forgive the Sandinistas
that you were so far away.

How will you know,
when you enter,
that this time,
I have no clothes on at all?
See how ruthless my love is?
I will also strip you
down to the bone,
even you,
with all your fashions and pretendings.

The old man
with his burlap sack of pine needles
made for us an altar,
a new kind of crèche
at the foot of the volcano.

Now you want me
to go back
to the old life,
as if after meeting God,
one is still applying
to a dating service.

I wanted to write a poem
about thinking about you all the time,
"A glass of wine long after moonrise
thinking of you,"
"Springtime of narcissus in the dusty alley
walking all by myself
thinking of you,"
but such a poem
could have no natural end.

In this life, then,
I love you,
this face, this body,
this life of yours.
You're such a poor man,
you have no others.

You thought I couldn't see
the light and shadow
of the ancient city
nor hear our footfalls
on the cobbled streets.
A haze of blue smoke
over the village
in the morning of tortillas.
Firecrackers at midnight
like a hailstorm on a tin roof—
I was inside of you
when the New Year began.

I do not know
how to reach you
except through these bodies
we must take off
again and again.
Rumi says,
"I want to kiss you,
the price of kissing is your life."[6]

---

6   From *Open Secrets, Versions of Rumi*, by John Moyne and Coleman Bark, Threshold Books, Putney, Vermont, 1984.

Service at the Earth Altar

Oh Great Spirit

In the name of Raven. In the name of Wolf. In the name of Whale. In the name of Elephant. In the name of Snake.

Who have taught us. Who have guided us. Who have sustained us. Who have healed us.

Please heal the animals.

In the name of Raven. In the name of Wolf. In the name of Whale. In the name of Elephant. In the name of Snake.

Whom we have slaughtered. Whom we have feared. Whom we have caged. Whom we have persecuted. Whom we have slandered. Whom we have cursed. Whom we have tortured.

Protect the animals.

In the name of Raven. In the name of Wolf. In the name of Whale. In the name of Elephant. In the name of Snake.

Whose habitat we have stolen. Whose territory we have plundered. Whose feeding grounds we have paved and netted. Whose domain we have poisoned. Whose food we have eaten. Whose young we have killed. Whose lives and ways of life we threaten.

Restore the animals.

In the name of Raven. In the name of Wolf. In the name of Whale. In the name of Elephant. In the name of Snake.

Forgive us. Have mercy. May the animals return. Not as a resurrection but as living beings. Here. On earth. On this earth that is also theirs.

Oh Great Spirit. Heal the animals. Protect the animals. Restore the animals.

Our lives will also be healed. Our souls will be protected. Our spirits will be restored.

Oh Spirit of Raven. Oh Spirit of Wolf. Oh Spirit of Whale. Oh Spirit of Elephant. Oh Spirit of Snake.

Teach us, again, how to live.

Akasha

On the dawn of her dying,
I was awakened
in another country
by the loon who showed herself,
finally, after calling, then hiding for days.
The sun burnished the sky
in astonishments of silver and bronze,
the grass turned radiant green
as the light made its pointed way toward me.
So I prayed,
"As I shall die too,
may I also die in beauty."

The Buddha of the Beasts

for Greg, and Timber Wolf

You arrived after howling alone for days. At first, companion to the other wolf, you lived in the animal realm and busied yourself with that domestic life. Then at the moment when you lost your mate, we found your territory. Perhaps you are the last wolf to wander in such hills.

You are the gift from my son. Your presence breaks that silence between us. You are everything we cannot speak about, but he has always known my longing for the wild thing is greater than my fear.

Three times when I walked to the river, at dusk, I broke the spider net gleaming over the path between the two trees. We call you the Buddha Wolf, watching the play of light as you bound between the worlds.

This is what I know about you: I cannot break your will. You will not be alone and you must be free. You are absolute and generous about your territory. The howl is more than an acknowledgement of the Moon. Every living thing, but one, is fluent in the language of the Great Heart.

It is a half mile downhill through the dark shade of the second growth redwoods to the river. After a hundred and fifty years, the grove which was desecrated is somewhat restored. There has been time for timbers to fall, for the sycamore, pine, laurel to turn about each other. What had been there for centuries is now present only in the wind, in the great shadow of the invisible limb toward which we are all climbing.

Now when I come to the river, the Great Blue Heron is waiting. He walks upstream while I follow his rhythm along the path. I say the names of the animals, not to separate myself, but as one repeats a rosary of preservation.

I liberate a self like one carves a stone, I excavate it from a garbage dump, from the detritus of culture, from the axe of expectation, from demand and sorrow. This unexpected self emerges from that compost like a sapling from the rotting stump of an old redwood. Even as I age, there is something in me becoming a girl. A stump that was cut down, flourishes again.

The first dog I ever had was a wanderer, came home smelling of fish oil, rotting food, covered with muck. I did not dare follow him then. You are old. Sometimes in the damp winters you limp. The hip is slow. It is an effort for your lungs to take in the breath and let it go. Still there is a deepening circle of light around your arcane silence, you gather it to you the ways the trees I love gather the night. In the order of things, it is easier for the gods to live in a tree or in a four-legged creature than in a person. I always wonder how a Buddha Wolf will die.

We can only heal so much. Some of what is broken in me will always be broken. Some grief is irreparable. You will die with or without a flash of lightning. The thousand-year-old trees will not return in the lifetimes of my species.

Still, I did not expect that ultimately you would be my mate. The girl I was did not guess she would become the gray wild-haired witch of the hill. Speaking the languages of beasts and trees was not how I imagined my life.

Do Not Tell Me What You Know

Do not tell me what you know.
Lead me by the hand
to the place we call
"This Is Beyond Me,"
where great and graceful creatures
cavort and lament.

In our silence,
voices we do not understand
become transparent,
the elegy of the humpback whale
and the invocation of the wolf
cross the boundaries between
here and there,
so that the Divine
without shape or determination
can inhabit the plumage
of the snowy owl
or infiltrate the secret code
of the elephant
as she maps the savanna,
resounding her own
subsonic Gloria and Te Deum.

Bears in the Snow

After the knowledge that the polar bear
who must live on ice, is drowning
as her ice floe melts before it makes its way
to land, seventy miles away, I wonder
what it serves to put one word after another
on the white page, even like this,
as last night's snow storm drips
in long, luminescent streaks
from the porch down to the earth
and slithers down the hill
to the streambed.

What was gathered
through the blessing of the storm
is undoing itself.
Even on the mountain
the white cache of water
disperses. We do not know
what the black bear will drink,
or whether there will be berries
when the summer comes,
or words that meet the moment
as divine whiteness
entirely disappears.

Losses

The year I didn't climb the ridge,
the house slipped away from me
as if all the winter waters had
finally undermined the foundation,
and neither love nor will
neither virtue, nor good intentions,
could hold it back.
It floated away on yellow feet
of abandoned chickens;
Baba Yar, the scrawny witch,
thrice twirled the house about
in watery vengeance,
and everything I'd given,
and I'd given everything,
was not enough.

I was aware
of the great insufficiency
in the universe,
admitted my love was incapable
of holding on to the impossible,
although the olive tree
I'd planted on the knoll for magic,
flourished most commonly
after losing its leaves,
but then it too plunged
into the ravine.

She came, as they say,
in a whirlwind,
leaves spun, the house groaned
as it tumbled.
Every hook to the invisible
I'd relied on
was undone, all offerings,
spells and contracts vitiated.
I saw the losses in the calm
of the morning,
mud burying the stars,
the clouds marching through the valley,
like a file of dead men.

At the Summit

of Mt. Pinos
is a flat stone
that has been warmed
all day by the sun.

I lie down and
offer my heart.
It is taken
again and again.

And yet,
I am not
without my heart.

What Shakes Me

After breath and light,
everything given to us
from below,
even fire
falling again
out of the sky,
into her dark body.

Nothing is built until stone
is quarried
or her great arms felled;
cities ground
from her pressed bones.
In Peruvian mines,
each vein
named for
a great whore.

Before the quake,
heaven aglow
from pressed quartz.
My sign is Earth.
The Magi says,
"Live in rubble for a year."

Where am I going
before I return
to myself?

Alchemy

This clay
I call my life
has a mouth.
To it,
I put my mouth
begging it to breathe.
Outside the circle,
the gods howl
their own pain without hands.
These shadows
want a body,
need to walk on feet,
to wake up in the rumple of sheets
about their shapes.

Having traveled the longing
of wishing to be with what dies,
I must walk
two stairs of vision into myself
beginning here,
in this density,
this heaviness of earth and water.

For centuries
men also worked
intractable heavy lead,
but then
the golem,
pounded from his own darkness,
lumbered forth.

Now, from the blind outside
of language,
we are called to the task again,
to bring breath
to these mouths
which do not know
their own names,
to the dream,
waiting for its own body,
while all of us prowl the centuries
with our teeth clenched.

What serves us,
this clay,
if it will not drink
from the river?

Four of Stones: The Power of the Earth

In a moment of despair, the augury speaks of the power of the earth. On this day, after incessant rains wore away the ground the way misery and fear erode the heart, the sweet waters, grim with debris, muddied, continued their way to the ocean, oily dark, unsafe, no longer the one we were traveling toward, no longer the water we dreamed as sanctuary to everything that lives.

We go where we have to go. Water flows downhill and cannot stop itself even if it can see from its snowy vantage that it will soon be at one with the dolphins beaching themselves and the hapless grebe sticky with tar. Pure, white, icy, it comes from afar, from the snowfields and the translucent glaciers shining with first light, and descending, helpless, bound to us, comrades in a chain gang, hitting the damned hammer of itself into the hapless earth, again and again and then it's in the muck.

Knowing gloom as the great enemy of possibility, I clutch the tree we call Hecate, an old one, that could have, like its companion, plummeted, but hasn't plunged into the ravine as great rocks tumble from the escarpment. The tree's gnarled root extends itself into the emptiness, a green figure, surprisingly a girl, a dryad on a tightrope, balancing against all odds.

I grasp the tree and beg for wisdom, imagining prayer winging across the entire expanse of America to the dispirited dolphins singing a song the winds carry westward. Gaining hope from their own music that somehow we hear and learn and carry, they turn to some new depths the tsunamis will open that will refresh them even so. A spirit shakes me, a wave breaking, dashing me to the grassy ocean floor before I can rise in a cetacean spin to the surface and breathe. I do not name what I do not understand; the song is halting and rough on these lungs filling with salt water.

Then I come home, righting the bluebird house that fell over in the wind, see the wolves gracefully lounging across the threshold, enter, throw the windows open, observe the first spring fly, spider, moth, lizard, all so young, beginners at this life, carrying, who knows what wisdom age cannot imagine as they scamper delighted and oblivious through this sudden new day.

This is when the augury comes: Four of Stones: The Power of the Earth[7] and also Shake/Rousing.[8] I do not know yet what it says, having paused to write first what it is certain to address, perhaps to ease. Healing would be too much to ask.

> An ancient tree roots in the underworld and branches in heaven.
> Thunder is a great shock coming from beneath,
> The rousing sun, green, wood, spring's beginning,

7   Four of Stones, "The Power of the Earth," from *The Haindl Tarot, The Minor Arcana*, Rachell Pollack, New Page Books, Franklin Lakes, NJ, pages 135–138.
8   "51 Shake/Rousing," from *Total I Ching: Myths for Change*, Stephan Karcher, Time Warner Books, London UK, pages 362–364.

Waking the sleeping insects.
The power of the earth is the voice of God.
Fear is inevitable before the hurricane and the tree of vision.
The omen speaks: Re-imagine and begin again,
The old ones have known this ten thousand years.

The presence of God will not save us but it will save the world. The mountain rises out of the magma. The melting ice refreshes the sea. We do not know the future uses of the oils that spew upward through the cracks in the earth. Before the skies darken, a thousand new effulgent greens burnish in the Hiroshima light of the setting sun.

A long sleep is inevitable. A coma of time stretches before us. Then they will come again, the small ones, born of fathers and mothers we will never know. Shapes we do not recognize chattering in unknown languages in our dreams of an incomprehensible future. They are like the lizard, the fly, the moth and the tiniest spider that race in hermetic script across the surface of the mind. Despair disperses in the dust storm and the whirlwind. What more comfort is wanted than knowing that the power of the earth is greater than we?

I fall, one falls down, before the earth trembler and the thunder beings, and even in such despair, open the heart. Then the fog comes in from the sea, a calming poultice for the burning light. The tree holds to its perch like an eagle to its aerie and those trees that fell root deeper into the saturated earth. Languages we have not yet learned come on the wind. Dolphin, far away, leap; we have to know the song is sung to us. Auguries, arrows from another world, strike us awake.

Leavings

I want what is left:
the tea leaves, the soiled images on cards,
the gasp of words as meaning slips away,
the rinds of the alphabet,
the chewed poems of prisoners,
the bones and the skeletons,
the secretions, the shattered sperm,
the spilled blood,
broken ova, the phlegm and the cough.

It has always been women's work to prepare the corpse.

But, I will not make a corpse from these elements,
I will make a child.
I will make you such a rose of a child,
a rose of a child held in the crook
of the dark hand of a dead branch,
I will make you a child shining
like an angel from these elements of dark,
and the child will sing.

This is what we have.
This is what we have to work with.

So give them to me,
first, your dead, moldering
in the dreadful heat of your deserted cities,
then, give me the iron birds in the sky,
with their demented warbling,
last, I want your radiant soil
with its eternal shimmer,
give me everything mangled and bruised,
and I will make a light of it to make you weep,
and we will have rain,
and begin again.

The leaves come down. The late yellow of winter, the color leached from the leaf. Leaves fall. Bougainvillaea withers, orange leaves curling from the frost. The towhee nests here this winter, instead of flying on. This transient visitor has become a resident.

Mockingbirds also build their nests. The starlings have arrived, swallows, flycatchers, thrashers, finches, mourning doves, robins, sparrows, titmice, for this sanctuary of a bit of water in a broken bowl. I look for them in the morning, at dusk, and at night, listening for their warning songs. Their presence a warning presence, their beauty, ominous, in our neighborhood.

The weather has changed. The birds gather, come closer to the house. The shy quail fly into the garden, an eddy in the non-existent wind. A brown feather drops between the limbs of the trees. The dust rises a little and falls.

There is neither thunder nor lightning. If there is sound it is only the scratch of thistles, some small thirsty rodent dragging itself across a twig or the brittle sage leaning into the rock. A dry season without wisdom. The bark peels off the trunk, a sheaf of skin from a burned body. The rust smoke from the earth chimney spreads through the galaxy.

The task is to learn from the animals. And to learn from them is to provide for them, that is to preserve their territory, that is to withdraw, as the Ein Sof withdrew for the sake of creation.

To withdraw. To pull in one's horns. To lower the voice. To take up less room. To give the yard to the wolves. To offer the apricots to the birds. To put out water for the jay. To invite the deer. To stop on the road for the coyote to pass. To allow the snake its rock, to rejoice in the grizzly by the fence posts. To learn the names of the animals and the names of the stars. This is what it has come to. This is the end of the poppies and the eucalyptus, the tulips and the golden fish. This is the end. A dull rust, an oak leaf bleached of its color, a sky gray and smudged. We had thought it would be different. We had thought we would die in a ruby blaze of fire or be preserved forever in the crystal glacial light passing over our feet. We had thought our death would be something glorious, the liquid of opals or the star sapphire alight in our eyes.

All day the ominous gray. The sky presses down upon us. There is weariness in heaven. A wind would bring rain, would stir up the salt water, would make the ocean dance, but nothing stirs under the gray fatigue except the birds.

But now it is late afternoon. Now they come again with their flickering shades of bronze and green, with their flashes of blue and yellow, with their asides of red and black. A fire in the garden on the wet wings of birds. A maelstrom of color. A waterfall of brown, orange and white. It would be ignoble all of it, mean and ignoble, if the garden weren't full of birds, their feathers, lemon and amber lights, under the still green leaves, these last flowers of the eucalyptus and the oak.

In the Morning   Walking

"In Pueblo societies a kind of ultimate democracy is practiced. Plants and animals are also people and through certain rituals and dances are given a place and voice in the political discussions of the humans. . . . What we must find a way to do, then, is incorporate the other people—what the Sioux Indians called the creeping people and the standing people and the flying people and the swimming people—into the councils of government."
—Gary Snyder, from *Turtle Island*

In the morning, everyone is asleep. The woods haven't awakened. Last night, I pushed the heart to the breaking point, wanting the poem to explode from the mad lady in a wild throw of cards and tea leaves or shamanic visions, tearing the spider webs from what is hidden, wanting to know what is coming and what has passed.

This morning, it is quiet. Even the dreams asleep in their walnut cradles and the evergreens pointing delicate tips toward the mist. Last night, I looked for fury and found it in a leaf where nothing is planned. Last night, we talked till dawn, two bottles of wine, whiskey, good dope, now black coffee in a glass under a tree. The bark peels off in ecstatic curls and underneath a true human limb, extended, mahogany and sensual entices me. I am shy of touching this stranger, madrone, and wait for an invitation.

This morning, rain only from the top of the redwoods when the wind shakes us. The banana slug, companion to these trees in its insistent yellow walk, like kelp, like certain burls of trees, like unopened lilies, this slug, a moving phallic wonder, extends across my path.

In the morning, the boy says, "The woods give me everything," thinking of the desert where he was given only rocks, insupportable heat, the curious lizard. Here there is water. And shade. And, if he has a gun, something alive to eat, a small fox or the bold deer that arrogantly stare into the loaded .22. Yet, in the distance, the rooster reminds us of barns and boundaries, a domestic clock that insists on morning. The song I follow is the bird I cannot see. Now my silence, so absolute, the hum of startled flies takes me by surprise.

This is the morning and my walk. I see only what the light falls on, though it's the dark I want to remember. The sun shines through, but what obstructs it, what it must bore through, engages me. This dark, like aboriginals and dreams, rejects the camera, says, "Nothing must be taken from the woods."

This same morning, the boy says, "Let me walk in the woods with you," thinks I know the way. The way my poet friend asked me to take her to the beach. Walking is something I know about. I want to walk across the Sierra Nevada, the Sierra Madre, the Andes, walking toward the southern tip. Let's calculate—assume ten thousand miles at twenty miles a day, it's only a couple of years, two hundred days to spare. Or if you want to walk with slugs, their pace is better, try ten miles a day, it's simpler and still ninety-five days to spare—that is three months sitting in place like native people unmoving, honoring the land—and three years walking. Just now I met a man who climbed the Andes for six weeks, without the language. It's only the pace that matters. If you weren't walking those three years what would you be doing?

Some mornings in these woods, I wake up talking, continue over eggs and orange juice and toasted muffins, securities from our common life. But sometimes, this morning, the woods call. Because there is no sun, nothing breaking through, only the wind, the slug, the jays, other rustlings in the undergrowth who do not ask permission. The woods teach us politics and co-existence, but we don't heed them. Whoever knows this secret, we put to death, then we bury them in crypts. Even the ghosts cannot return, night or morning, to tell us, and no vegetables from our wisdom, this deprivation even of the compost fire.

In the mornings, I am always hearing unexpected voices. The woman who stopped me, asking, "Are you a gypsy or another of those dark skinned people, like Indians?" I was buying a silver hand against the evil eye for someone who had given me his protection. Amulets keep us safe but only when we do not escalate the evil. Nothing can keep us indefinitely from the useless shade we cast.

The difference between the tree and the umbrella: the first, even this morning, lets through some of the light and rain. We are too absolute about our territory. Death could be the democratic grist, promises a temporary resurrection in a knowable form. For example, my body, returning as a mushroom, nestling under a fern who is the man I love. He and I running in long vines, morning glories, towards the sea. Passion flowers become fruit. We might be carrots together, squash. Life can be round as pumpkins. And death as bright. We're eaten—Thanksgiving—when you remember the Indians who tried to teach us this.

One morning, a conversation: I say, "There are only three good reasons for war. Food. Fertilizer. Religion." We don't even kill for God anymore, but for the hell of it. Hundreds of thousands. And since you won't eat my heart, then, at least let me astonish you, one morning, with my blossoms.

This morning, the woods, the mulch smell. Old sinking down, new pushing through. The old trees talking. A dead bird feeding some forest creatures, the common denominator of the species. The Native Americans are dead. Murdered. Yet, fortunately, buried bare in the earth. Something lurks in the trees, then, to give us warning.

Opening All the Doors to the Rain

Today the rain comes. A small knocking on the skylight at night, as if something mechanical is aflutter or a shy animal is cleaning its home.

The earth remembers, but not easily. At first the crust is adamant, lets nothing in, the water flows down the sides. Only gradually does the soil open, become permeable, let the rain slip between the stones. Then the clay slides over the bones of rock.

The mystery of rain. The sky, transparent and miraculous, falling toward the earth. The sky, given to us, offering itself, in the form of rain. The god descending, to be taken up or taken in.

When I was ten, I washed my hair in a fierce storm, water breaking over my head and streaming white down my body, a wraith of white foam about my ankles. I kept my face toward the sky long after the soap had disappeared, for the hammer of water upon my naked body.

I have been afraid to pray for rain. I do not know if we retain the right, given that we set fires in all our footprints. Let us not make promises we will not keep.

Once rain came to me in a dream in the form of dancers. I awakened frightened, but the next week I danced the rain dance; then it did rain. It was a satisfying coincidence. And then it rained again and continued to rain. And rain. I tried to forget the dream. I didn't dance again. I didn't call for rain.

Another time, it rained for days. The hill slid against the house. The water seeped in through the walls. In the morning, it seemed as if the bed was afloat, or the room itself was a solar barque taking us to our death. To die by water is said to be a gift of the gods.

Each summer, the river was brown and warm as the beginning of time at Canyon de Chelly. The river was always knee deep where the sheep graze the river grasses. But last summer, the river was dry as the canyon walls. The juniper drooped at the edge, the pinion pine parched, the wind dusty and unrelenting moaned through the stunted *milpa*. Bears came down from the hills looking for water. I asked for the dream to return as a sign, though I was afraid. But the dream did not return. I saw no dancers, not even in the clouds.

Today, rain returns. Mud slides. Steam blows off the wet fence during intermittent moments of sun. Small green grasses arise at the side of the road. Mist hovers about the edges of the mountains. The canyon glides again toward the sea. The wolves break open the door, dry themselves at the hearth. Little field mice scurry through the cabinets. The frogs that have lived in the closet move outside, singing. Bulbs bore through the soft earth, scent of narcissus, glimpses of hyacinth.

In the Beginning, after the flood there was a rainbow. Now, during the drought, this sweet interval of rain. But the question remains: Do we have a right to pray for rain? What can we offer before we take in the rain with our dry roots and open mouths, when the fires we are setting are seething on the horizon?

Vulture Medicine

There she sits on the dead tree,
black against the gray-pink clouds
as men gather to capture God
and confine her to a small preserve
out of our sight.

We know her best through legends
that say when all others failed,
this Great Mother pressed her forehead
against the sun,
pushing it against the sky
to save the earth from burning,
and so carries that mark
that red, bald head forever.

It is said
that when she cannot find
the dead to feed the little ones,
she will, like the pelican,
open her thigh
with her rapier tongue,
with the gentlest lick
slice skin, flesh, muscle
to offer her blood,
to those who will someday
be called to share her glorious fate.

The sun illuminating the southern limbs
has turned the dead tree on the mountain,
rising above all others,
into a fiery signature
where this vulture,
the great condor,
with the wingspread of an angel, sits.

She is not poisoned by the dead;
What we must not eat,
she eats for our sake.
But she is poisoned by our poisons
that twenty years ago took all her people,
save three, to the grave.

And still she comes to live among us
though it may kill her and all her young again.

Mut, Maat, Maat, Racham, Kadosh

I did not think such medicine
would come to me as a sign.
I say her name,
Mut, Great Mother,
Maat, the Cosmic Law
who weighs us against such a feather.
Racham.
To both the Arabs and the Jews
who war against each other,
she is the Compassionate One,
bearing yet another face of God.

Mut, Maat, Maat, Racham, Kadosh

She comes sweeping the sky,
her black feathers signing prayer
as they reach up.
It is my birthday,
The wind hums through the trees;
We call it, *ruach*,
the breath of God.

Vulture spirit
draws a single circle
a thousand feet above me,
perfect in the blue and gray and azure
of the holy sky; it is enough for me,
to know her from this stone circle
dedicated to the Great Mother,
where I sit praising the old ones,
and singing Blind Willie Johnson's
tune: *Just God, Nothing But God, Just God,*
until it's time to follow silence.

So the last third of my life begins.
The vulture does not speak, or call or sing.
She is the womb through which we pass.

The sun dissolves the clouds.
As the summer fire emerges,
she turns to face me,
lies down on a branch.
Such a narrow perch
becomes her bed; nothing more required.

It is not for us to say
what beauty is,
but to honor its black feathers
and terrible skull
when she appears.

I take what is given:
the means and measure of the vulture
is my medicine and I praise
the story telling of God.

Mut, Maat, Maat, Racham, Kadosh
Mut, Maat, Maat, Racham, Kadosh

Vulture

Vulture
on the dead
tree, black lightning
against a sky
of ashes and fire.
These sephirot
have opened
my heart,
boring in
with their endless
soaring.

MaNdlovu[9]

Suddenly, I am of a single mind extended
across an unknown geography,
imprinted, as if by a river, on the moment.
A mind held in unison by a large gray tribe
meandering in reverent concert
among trees, feasting on leaves.
One great eye reflecting blue
from the turn inward
toward the hidden sky that, again,
like an underground stream
continuously nourishes
what will appear after the dawn
bleaches away the mystery in which we rock
through the endless green dark.

I am drawn forward by the lattice,
by a concordance of light and intelligence
constituted from the unceasing and consonant
hum of cows and the inaudible bellow of bulls,
a web thrumming and gliding
along the pathways we remember
miles later or ages past.

I am, we are—
who can distinguish us?—
a gathering of souls, hulking and muddied,
large enough—if there is a purpose—
to carry the accumulated joy of centuries,
walking thus within each other's
particular knowing and delight.

This is our grace: To be a note
in the exact chord that animates creation,
the dissolve of all the rivers
that are both place and moment,
an ocean of mind moving
forward and back,

---

9   *MaNdlovu* is the word the Ndebele people of Zimbabwe use for female elephant. It is connected
in resonance with *Mambo Kadze*, the name for the deity that is both elephant, the Virgin Mary and
the Great Mother.

outside of any motion
contained within it.

This is particle and wave. How simple.
The merest conversation between us
becoming the essential drone
into which we gladly disappear.
A common music, a singular heavy tread,
ceaselessly carving a path,
for the waters tumbling invisibly
beneath.

I have always wanted to be with them, with you, so.
I have always wanted to be with them,
with you,
so.

Trees Walking to Water

She Brings Forth Green Leaves[10]

Something settles the tight
nest of the heart,
tree scooped out
for a running creature
O!   squirrel
O!   eye
tell me the forest chatter.

I think I must be the tree
but also the hole in it
pecked out by a sharp beak,

Or
am I the heart
that lives in the tree?
I am so aware of the movement,

the going back and forth,
the opening and closing.

---

10   Title from "Eye of the Stone," by Judith Minty.

The Trees Ask Me Home

soon
I'll sleep each night
with the breath of leaves
in the bed, the cough of eucalyptus,
the restless stirring of fig and lime,
There is so much life here,
rooster as alarm, hawk as sentinel,
coyote as guard, life
and ferment, death is close by.

When the human species deserted him,
tomatoes were what my father planted,
they were his true love.
With their imperative, he spent
weekends in the sun,
so I learned to talk to trees.
I see the song coming, a wing
out of the nest of bitterness,
light and dark. And further on,
those footsteps in the mulch,
that path through the new grove,
must be mine.

The story of my life
is the story of trees I've loved,
some are standing, some fell down.

Out of Old Wood Long Season[11]

When I was young, we burned the garden deliberately,
planted trees as if it were the holy land,
not the abandoned lot we could have
for back taxes if we had the money. The cherry tree
was white and brilliant and my father
put his writing table beneath it in the summer
when the fruit was amber in color,
rather like Tokay or sherry, rather like autumn.
That was his tree. It had the most light.
The momma tree, the lesser tree,
was the wormy peach by the arbor, striving
for the portion of sun that didn't fall
to the dark grape. Behind these, the apple
even more in the dark and bearing green
and sour fruit long after summer had collapsed.
This tree, the most ignored, belonged to me.

Later on my own land there was a maple tree
confined within a brick corral.
I think the tree was a young girl, her hands
up above her head, quite willing to be alone,
about the age that girls turn to horses.
There wasn't much to talk to, nothing more
than sparrows and in a rare March, a yellow bird
whose name I didn't ask, sudden and fleeting
as a daffodil. She put out her leaves,
for the bird, I suppose. I didn't mind
her distance and I didn't admire it either,
I thought it was simply curious, this maple
in my back yard, how far away she was.

---

11   Title from "Burning Against the Wind," by Judith Minty.

93

Who Lives in the Tree

She is Daphne, but look
Apollo is also caught
in the white bark,
the two twisting together at the root.
We thought he was in pursuit,
but when he reached the leaves
that are her hair,
she caught him in her embrace.
It was winter before he knew it;
the snow permitted a secret joining.

Knowing that she was afraid
and fear could be his loss,
he had chased her, but praying
the woods would take them both.

Afraid she would turn from him,
he would sit on the damp ground,
leaning against her mossy torso
as she grew silent
musing about the sky,
reaching away from him
like someone who over the years,
takes solitude as her lover.

Now they are one tree
by design.
He bends over
the arch of her belly,
the curved whinny of her neck,
the white parabola of her desire.

He watches as
she bends back,
lifts up to him.
The separate arc
of his trunk traces hers.
His eye following the cleft,
sees where he cannot hold her
despite his ardor.

His eye cannot see
where her branches
entangle him nightly,
that her leaves are fists
grasping his hair
in the shudder of wind.

Beech/Asherah

When you come upon it,
as if it were an accident,
the chance of a seed
falling from the chance
histories of seeds,
the chance histories
of atoms and molecules,

you see,
finally,
the tree to which you have been led
your entire life,
you see
another kind of script,

not the warning
of the handwriting on the wall
but the mystery of the ongoing beginning,
and then you know

it is worth everything
to decipher the holy
as inscribed,
and the sacred letters,

not to craft an independent creation
nor to impose your will,
but to companion what is written
within yourself.

At the feet of the tree
that once taught us,
you can learn this again.

Did you notice
that we walked
through
the holy apple orchard to get here?

Light on the Old Pine

The candle of the pine
has split off and fallen alongside the living tree,
and the light on the toppled trunk
is making candlelight of the needles,
so life and death are companions once again.
It may take the entire remaining life of the tree
for the fallen trunk to disappear into another living future.
Each day it offers more of itself up
but barely.
Nearby, a young pine has broken in half,
its upper trunk has severed, has become a limb
extending straight out
in places, still green.
Life persists through the narrowest channels.

This is what I count on:
that perpendicular limb and the broken ridgepole,
and, oh, yes, the light on the golden needles.

The Old Ones

Overnight,
through the relentless descent
of light, the trees
have become the old ones
bowed by the burden of brightness.

They sway with it,
teaching the rhythm of prayer.
I sway with them,
arms rising and falling,
finding a harmony
that must have tuned my mind
eons before I was born.

At the edge of the gloved needles,
the water is melting clear,
transparent nails
from the green hand.

It will snow again tonight,
the sky will turn gray-black
as white will fall out of the darkness.
We will rest in this in the morning.

Shadow of Fern

The toothy tiger shadow of fern
on the broad maple leaf vine,
wild in its original form,
gentle and hungry without malice.
I have been led,
by following the light,
to a triangle of fallen birch,
white bark curling
around trunks settling
into the earth in their own time.
I am, by design, in a prow,
rowing a boat across an ocean
I would not pretend to have discovered;
it is unknown to me,
and entirely green.

Another sign of the possibility
of a future. This is second
or third growth. Here
it seems so pristine, that is,
so much itself. Yet, here, also,
are so many clean, hewn trunks.
Numerous ones have been here
before me with saws,
making the smooth cuts
that require less effort than axes,
and take so much more than is needed.

Still, the trees return, forming
a thicket amidst the ferns.
Moose has been here recently,
and bear has left
fresh notations on the trees
to be divined.

I had thought
I had come here
to make alliances,
but I understand
that I have come
to be a servant.

This is what I know
so early on this first day
of being almost entirely alone.

A kind man and woman
came to hang a hammock
between the trees.
When they left,
I knew I was alone,
and so very grateful
to have been led
so soon to some
beginning of not knowing,
that will, no doubt deepen,
as the woods do,
until I am further
than I have ever been—
already this is true—
into what exists
entirely in the habitat
of what are not
the ways of my species.

And there—
But who can say anything?—
if I can disappear myself,
I may also,
as I know myself, disappear,
the way wind disappears,
in order finally to know, in this life,
something of what is.

Singing to the Dead

I Can See the Dead Crossed Limbs Longing Again for the Universe[12]

The snow we've smelled in the air,
pointing anxious nostrils to
the blood moon, falls finally with
the temperature, and we will be buried
today, this Sunday of beginnings.
It tramples with its white hooves
even on this site of holy water
bubbling up to heal us, hot
with the stinking sulphur breath of
the underworlders. This is the
frost month, what appears to descend
is sent in fact from below,
and we cannot hide the error
of even a single pomegranate seed
in this absolute whiteness.

It is under these white covers
that I meet the hell maiden,
the old bitch without teeth, the drawer
of the waters, the one
I call a crone though she is not
thin enough in her shaking flanks.
Her face is pitted with all
the diseases of our nightmares,
the boils, pustules, leprous
embellishments, the plagues
and smallpox of our fears. She
is the one who draws the holy water,
the sacred water bubbling up
about my body in the pristine enamel tub,
in this tiled ivory vaulted chamber,
this hospice for the dying, erected
on holy ground.

She, the hag, helps me out
of the bath, wraps me in hot sheets,
winding me down to the hell fires,
then rubbing my body with her hide
hard hands, preparing me as one
prepares a corpse to last. I want

---

12   Title from "Under the Maud Moon," in *The Book of Nightmares* by Galway Kinnell.

to say, "You lie down on this
gurney and I'll stretch your muscles
with oil," but each of us goes
to our death in our own time.
I give her my body, fresh from the bath
of these holy waters as the horn
of her finger presses into my breast.
I do not know if life is possible
in this resurrection, yet
I take in her white snort of animal breath.
Wherever the snow lunges, I follow, determined
to love this damned bull in all these
disguises.

Bird Calls

In the morning,
it is a small death,
one stone calling
to another
as the heart closes.
If the air shuddered
when the bird plummeted,
no sound was uttered.

This time a yellow claw
scratched the wind.
Only bodies want to die. Ghosts
prefer the dark corners,
becoming the snatch
of dream fading
in the morning sun.
This bird
had a song once, now
only this odd plumage
at my fear.

    If I say,
    I want to die,
    it is because
    death is so lonely
    without us.

Dreaming the Road

It wasn't a dream, unless we shared it open-eyed, your car exploding into dream car, driving us further than we understood. Dreaming the road, we might dream only the first red stroke on a preliminary map, dream the cartographer, the engineer, and the man at the curve of the road with the sign, *Stop.*

It wasn't a dream, it wasn't the afternoon road, the trees light-speckled, it was bark and leaf, it was. . . . Moon stopped us, or wind, and a mud-stained pine root rose ghostly across our way. Stopped as in a dream, we stopped on the divided road and waited to build the road.

> I see,
> you see,
> the squirrel
> dragging her dead mate across the road.

There is the poem.

We do not dream this and we do not plunge into sorrow. Friendship is not prepared for what we see. We shift in the car from each other. This is a vision for lovers: the small creature, hobbled by her burden, teeth in the tail and claws too small to carry, insists her way across the road.

The two of them, the live one and the dead one, make their way to some leaf-mulched grave.

We stop and wait, then she—'He,' you say—skitters away, frightened by the shadows we cast, and we become pallbearers with twigs. "Do we dare?" you ask, and lay him—'Her,' you say—under a tree. And then drive on.

It might have been a car that didn't stop, we say. What can friendship manage? Lovers might live the dream and build a temple at the sight of god in the afternoon dragging the lover back to the dark heart. But we did not dream this. The road was a road. We had to be cautious of our scent. Soon the ants would come.

I know this story and the irrevocable order of things.

Silence for My Father

This is the silence around the poem of the death of my father.
This is the silence before the poem.

While my father was dying, the Challenger was exploding on TV
Again and again. I watched it happen. In his hospital room,
I followed his breath. Then it stopped.

This is the silence in a poem about the dying of the father.

We're burning the earth. We're burning the sky.

Here is another silence in the middle of the poem about the immolation of the Fathers.

The pyres of bodies in Saigon.
The burned air
The charred limbs.
Ash.
Rancid flames.
Heat
Light
Fire
                    We turn away.

Here is another silence within the poem about the burial of the fire.

When my father died, the rains poured down the moment I picked up the shovel of earth.
I staggered under the weight of the water.

Another silence please.

I have always wanted to be a woman of fire.
I will have to learn how to rain.
Gently, I will learn how to rain.

I have set fire to your green fields,
May I be water to your burning lands.

Please join me in this last silence at the end of the poem of fire.

Thorn

Everything dies. Without you
I saw one million flamingos

ignite a lake in Africa.
The same darkness

descended everywhere.
When you dropped your body,

I hoped you would tremble
for the beak of God.

Why did we wash you three times
tearing off the girl's white dress

to swaddle you in an austere shroud?
Some say, dying, not death, teaches.

You gained nothing
from that reduction.

Months in the narrow foxhole of disease—
you dug it; we filled it in.

My father is thin as you were
in his hospital bed,

both of you let everything go,
care for nothing

except that barbed hook—
life.

It grabbed you like a thorn
until you begged me, "Pull it out."

Who Knows What the Thirst Is For

I imagine my own death:
I will want something to drink.

Her buttocks ran like mud.

Her legs were the broken
sticks of the Camps;
she hid them from her sons.

The last day,

she didn't want to see them, or
they couldn't see her
rising like mist.

This life, the chimney.

Whoever cannot imagine Hiroshima
cannot know *oven, shower* or *soap.*

Now her narrow ring
fits the finger of my right hand.

A bone was all
Hansel had for protection.

My death will be simple,
I will not be distracted,

I will have had enough practice
to drink the water
and know everything.

At Kealakekua Bay

Under the mountain,
where the royal bones were buried
by a commoner,
cut loose,
then dropped into the sea,

a bleached frond meets a white stone
in ribs and skull of colt,

so we understand
the body,
how we die,

sacrifice,
regret,
betrayal,

as paper leaves
dissolve before our eyes.

The Cave

Death is a dark cave
that, expanding,
stretches the heart open.
Afterwards, it never closes.
We do not enter into it
so much as it opens in us, wide.
We become it,
the passageway,
through which
we know what we know
see what we see,
are, finally, who we must be.

Ice of Hope

This first day of winter, a small bird, ice of hope, wings through the dull desert brush. Cavorting ravens mark ice floes in the snow tinged sky to the far north. Fading light is faintly stroking the stone flanks of animals, elephants and whales, slow as time; the great, gray deliberate boulders will remain no matter what we do.

I have just lost the one, who stood between me and mortality. Only these stones now as a bulwark.

We are one day out of the darkness and the moon is full tonight. Running to these stone creatures I love, whose company I crave, I fall before a small bush resplendent with pink flowers. Prostrate, I remember this fire pink has come to us in dreams as a sign of wonder. This is so modest a flower, I could have missed it, except that it is winter and the wind has ice on its breath, and I fall before it, fall before what could have been a spring bloom, a summer blossom, fuller still, shaded by its tawny, tough, serrated, scratchy leaves.

But it is winter. I am brought to my knees. This way I begin this season of the dark while overhead, the dark clouds of the north open their bodies to the setting sun and burn.

The old man had been stubborn about his dying, but even he could not redeem us, could not undo the curses and the broken covenants with Ice and Fire. And yet, salamanders in the sky, the intemperate pink flower, the ice of hope.

No Roots Are Mine[13]

It wasn't that he looked back
but that he was a singer.
His mouth opened
just then
to her name;
Eurydice
was the song on his lips.
Enchant is to be in song.
Some cannot leave the dark
and he wouldn't follow her,
not even singing.

---

13 Title from "Now It Is Clear," in *The Carrier of Ladders*, by W. S. Merwin.

Feasting the Dead

They come to us more often now,
the dead, because we are more willing
to entertain them or because
they cannot bear to see everything
they lived for, burn.
Here they are, the engineers and architects,
the generals and scientists who imagined
only goodness but didn't see far enough.
And here are the others,
the mountain of what we would call poor souls
who ate stones and mutton and rough bread,
nothing like our own. Among them, here
and there, the poets who cared for nothing but words,
and see what has become of them. They move
skillfully through all the lines of the dead, no strangers
to lost hopes, and tap a rounded shoulder,
bow to someone's ghost. They are silent now, of course,
and yet encourage us to do as they did,
put one word before the other. Not for posterity,
though they didn't know it then, not for fame,
but for the exercise of the forced march.
No matter how one suffered, still
as long as we were marching,
we were alive.

Cathleen Ni Houlihan Burke

June 23, 1951–September 20, 1994

I have
a strong voice
Here.

Mercy,
I could never
accept
or understand,
I have
Here.

Mary,
to whom
I would not
pray,
is
Here.

Peace,
I never knew,
is Here
as well.

I was
Cathleen Ni Houlihan,
and I was
looking
for my
four beautiful
green fields.

That is,
I was looking
for my life

The beauty
you love
so much
comes
from the
violent dark.

You always
forget.

Here,
we call it
Grace,
that forgetting.

The mystery
you stumbled upon:
Now,
I will not
fade.

The body matters,
so does time.
Do not be
frivolous.
Be fierce
as we are
Here.

I could not
stay,
I could not
let myself
be loved
enough.
Some grief
cannot
be expunged.

Those lost
four fields,
I had nowhere
to walk.

Learn
the ruthless
presence
of the other side
through me.

Keep your eyes
open,
look across
Here.
Be fearless.

I do not mean,
do not
be afraid,
I do not mean
there is
nothing to fear,

I mean
be fearless.

I mean
I am
Here.

Calling a Mother with Advice for the Duat

In Honor of Nebt-Het

There are words, mother,
that you will need to learn
that bring the dead back to life.
These are not the words of Creation:
In the Beginning,
but the words of undoing:
In the end.

A spell is to be disassembled,
each word cleansed in a river
that flows backwards in time
to another water for which
we do not have a name.
This is your task: Find the Name.

This is how you begin:
First, take the filaments
that you spun
from words,
take everything that came of them,
and speak backwards,
undo the spell they cast.

Take these words
as if they are a tangled
skein of silk and wash them
the way you may have dreamed
of washing your hair in a river
when you were a young girl
and thought about angels.

Let the light unfold,
return to the river
like so many flakes of gold.
Goldie, they called you briefly,
though you were afraid of the name,
so took Bella, meaning beautiful.
It is the same name
but one name belongs to one world,
and the other name to this world,

and now you are hovering alongside
the name you were afraid to wear.

Now for the river:
It is a dry river.
It begins in the desert
and it ends in the desert.
How will you wash your
name in a river which
cannot flow?

You will have to weep the river,
a river of salt that becomes
a lake of sweet water
burrowing down
into the center of the
earth and then rising
again to our feet
and we drink from it.

This then is what you
must do:
You must weep
from your own body,
washing your own life
reducing it to grains
of sand, glimmers,
brief and eternal lights.
By the time
you have finished weeping,
you will be dissolved
in the waters of life
that sustain us,
and then you will know
the name of the river
because you will know
the loss of
your name.

Do not be afraid.
Others have gone before you

and you yourself
came forth out of such waters.
The waters of the womb—
what do you think are their source?
Mother, birth us now.
It is your turn
to be the mother of the waters of sorrow.

The Death of the Wolf

I begin to dig the grave; the joy of the pickaxe against the stone, that splintering that only comes when metal strikes and what seems so solid is sheared.

She slept beside him all night. Her vigil now, as he had slept beside her, turning her to breathe. Those times when she was passing over to this side with equal struggle, crossing here from death, he found her, as she found him, under the tree, among the leaves. Their brokenness mended each other. The two serrated halves fit.

To glue one part to another, you must roughen the surface first. That which is smooth, or perfect, cannot fit against another.

You bring the rain. Your dying breaks the clouds. The language of the sky drums upon the leaves and yellow blossoms of the acacia.

You are hovering about me. I can feel you in my nostrils, everywhere, every time I breathe. The howl, both mournful and ecstatic, echoes. The death of the wolf, but not the death of the spirit.

There is a grief which has no earthly counterpart, though they say, here, this place, earth, is the only place where death exists. This means, there is no life anywhere else. This means this place, this earth, is death's house.

It was something like a star going out or being born. That electric shudder, your entire body trembling, the current rushing also through my heart, your spirit shaking off the flesh. I cannot believe it is the end of love. You always tended us so well.

"The spirit is gone," I said, "but he is still alive." And then, moments later, "He is dead."

In the afternoon, we knew a star had appeared somewhere in the universe. The great darkness punctured by a new light. I expect nothing less than such a flame from you, a sun that will burn ten billion years. Until we're all aflame or all put out.

A great beauty descended upon you in your death. The grace of your entire life coalescing into a moment of perfect sleep. I passed my hand over your yellow eyes that had become stones. In the morning, you moved, your belly rising with the first motions of the universe, the gases within you burning.

The other wolf stood at the edge and pushed dirt onto you with her nose. Now you are shaking the branches of the olive tree that will root about your bones. Your body, in the earth, on the knoll where we are permitted to bury only my ashes.

When I die, they will say, "She gave the wild a home. A wolf lived with her."

The olive leaf is dark on one side and full of light on the other.

When I Am Dying

When I am dying,
someone will go home because she is tired,
or they will miss the call, or look away,
or he will momentarily follow a thought,
and we will miss the exact moment of separation
when I will be whirled elsewhere.
Beyond does not describe it, for we believe we have gone there,
while this will be further than anywhere any of us have ever been.
Though you thought to go with me
some of the journey
because we have been of one mind for our lifetimes,
even you will be deceived by the visible,
by an explosion or the stillness of breath,
by blood, carnage, a blast of silence not unlike a bomb
leaving a crater in the earth.

That will be it.
My departure will have become familiar
through discussions of pulses, inhalations, exhalations and secretions,
politics, murders, or other disasters,
as if all of you had calculated these rhythms before,
while I will be uniquely, and for the very first time,
where I have never been before
and could not imagine.
Then separate,
though we have refused to be so our entire lives,
we will rely on grief,
on becoming a mad woman, a mad man,
on a gust of wind under the door,
any bitter sudden cold will remind you
of the swirling emptiness always between us,
and so between us now.

It's Time

Just when
it seems that we've shaped
it so,
it's time
to open the hand
—moth in the palm—
purse lips
          blow.

Walking with Neruda

In 1988, I imagined a relationship with Neruda.
This is a record of that friendship.

Walking with Neruda

Pablo Neruda, I introduce myself as the one who is behind you. I sleep under your feet. I walk where you walked. Perhaps I walked to Chile, for since I learned your name, I could do nothing but walk after you. After I read your poems, I walked in my sleep.

In Chile, I pursued you. When you took walks, I followed you to know how a poet walks. When you walked with your wife, I followed the two of you. I noticed when you stopped, when you spoke to each other, when you were silent. I had to learn from the tone of your back when you were looking inward, when you were looking out. I was determined to know how you turned what you came upon into words.

I followed you for weeks. You allowed me the dignity of being unacknowledged. I fell in beside you after I had followed you day after day in the rain. Did you love the world so much that bitter cold and wind could not dissuade you from pursuing it?

I began to believe that I would learn everything if I watched you walk, even if I never had read a single poem you wrote, or never looked into your face. I began to believe that you were your back, the sound of your feet, the route you chose. You were no more—but no less—than your consistent deliberate habit of walking. You were your feet, despite the newspaper headlines, visiting dignitaries, urgent telephone calls, coups, persecutions and all siren songs.

One day when your feet became the universe itself, I fell in alongside you. You didn't speak; you were always the poet. Once, I tripped and you put out your hand to steady me, but this also without a word. And once—before we had spoken a word—you tipped your hat, a trifle mischievously, I thought, as you went into the house. After a while, I liked to think you were waiting for me each day, that you hesitated just a moment at the door, looking about without looking, before you set out for the sea.

I wanted to be your lover, your sister and your shadow. I wanted to be the paper you wrote upon and the air you breathed. I wanted to know everything without interfering or deflecting you in the slightest from the splendid and eloquent isolation of your stride. If I could, I would have been the road extending myself in rock and sand to the print of your feet, rolling endlessly under you.

Finally, I spoke. You said, "Don't speak. Not here. Not now. Coffee is for speaking, also *aguardiente*. Speech is best at five in the afternoon with a little brandy. Also it is good to speak after ten at night, accompanied by *sopa de mariscos* and over an extraordinary Chilean *vin ordinaire*. But while walking in the rain and fog, it is best to be silent. Here poems are born into words only if nothing is said."

I listened. I nodded to indicate I'd understood what you said. You saw my hunger. You passed a few dry twigs to me, some yellow and orange leaves, the black stones of Isla Negra. At the knees of the sea, you bent down, straining your portly body, to dip your fingers into the foam and press the salt water to my lips. It occurred to me to eat everything you gave me, even soil, to ingest the elements of earth from which you made poems. I began to understand the terrifying and necessary intimacy with the world which poetry requires.

When you felt that I was becoming deeply acquainted with silence, when you saw that I was no longer speaking words in my mind, when you saw that I could forget words altogether for miles at a time, you invited me into your house.

Bienvenido

Speaking with Neruda

I had imagined conversation. Surely, Neruda was one of the great talkers. I thought I needed that talk. After all, I came to him frightened, a dumb teenage girl with shaking hands, essentially insecure about language. Moses, who is in my lineage, put coals in his mouth and stuttered afterwards, while I imagined doves flying out of Pablo's mouth whenever he spoke. *Palomas. Palomas blancas* quivering wings. Words like startled feathers. *Un nido* of burning sentences.

I imagined long literary evenings, odes intoned to the beat of the *charanga*, gossip long as gallows, speeches pregnant with clouds and grammatic shadows. *La noche escondida, la mascara* of painted *palabras,* lucid *pajaros de la anochecida.*

He gave me a blank piece of paper. "Dare," he laughed.

When I entered his day room whirring white doves, their eyes *brilliantes entre dos luces de cobre*, settled into their golden cages. I called to them, "Coo, coo." My breath smudged the night with coal dust, *Negra y pesada.*

If I write this, if I dare to imagine the moment—as I have imagined others—where a man or a woman who had no prior existence suddenly grow ruddy with the breath of life on the page—if I dare to imagine this: myself, this poet named Pablo Neruda, the two of us together in a room—*viviendonos*—he hasn't died yet—poetry is still possible—it is raining in the south of Chile. . . . I know the landscape. *La lluvia* of hope . . .

A woman who writes a word down is not the same as one who does not.

When I was not yet twenty-four, I followed Pablo Neruda, the world's greatest poet, into his house.

He said, "A woman rarely becomes a poet because the fathers tell her to keep her body closed and the mothers agree. If you want to write, you will have to be as open as the sea. *Apertura lluviosa.*" He said, "Live in my house for a month and don't speak. *Mi casa es tu casa—miento incommunicado.*"

Something in the Belly

I wanted to have a poem and I was pregnant. I was very thin. As if I'd lived on air. A poet must be able to live on air, but a mother must not attempt it. My mother wanted me to buy a set of matching pots, Wearever aluminum, like the ones she had. They were heavy and had well fitting lids so my suppers wouldn't burn. My husband wanted me to give dinner parties. John F. Kennedy was running for office.

I sensed danger. Kennedy wasn't against the Bomb or for nuclear disarmament. I joined SANE at its inception. Also Concerned Scientists. I spoke with Linus Pauling and encouraged my husband to help his partner organize Physicians for Social Responsibility.

There was a baby in my belly. I wanted to write poems. I had a crazy idea that a woman could write a real novel, the kind that shook the world. I hallucinated that a woman could be a poet, but she would have to be free. I couldn't imagine that freedom for myself even though I could see it in Isla Negra when I followed Pablo Neruda. I could see it in the way he walked. Even if he were walking inside a dictatorship, among guns, soldiers and spies, there was nothing between him and his vision. Anything he saw, he was able to take into himself—there was no sight, no image, no vision to which he didn't feel entitled. In his heart, everything—everything—belonged to him. Pablo Neruda was—more than anything—a poet, and so he was an entitled man.

I was a woman and entitled to nothing. I had nothing except a husband, a rented house, a set of pots, living room furniture, a frenzy of obligations, credit cards, anxious relatives, too many acquaintances, a gift of future diaper service, two telephones, no time to read, a plastic wrapped cookbook of recipes gleaned from the pages of the *New York Times*, and a hunger, a terrible hunger for the unimaginable, unlimited freedom of being a poet, and a baby in my belly.

I would have called Pablo long distance if I had the courage, if I had the ability to speak Spanish fluently, if we had ever talked about real things. But, what would a man know about a baby in the belly? And what did it matter if there were to be one poet more or less in the world when so many in his country were dying?

I woke up one morning and thought—I can't have this child. My husband said, "You'll have to get a job after it's born so we can buy a house. You'll need an advanced degree so you can do something." I thought, I can't. I have to write poems. My mother found a crib. Someone painted it white. A friend sent a pastel mobile with tame wood animals. I thought about blue curtains, making bedspreads, and abortions.

Pablo was silent. He was walking so far away from me, I couldn't hear him. My husband objected to donating more free medical care to the Black Panthers. I tried to make *dolmades* from scratch and located grape leaves preserved in brine at the Boys' Market twenty miles away. I organized a write-in campaign for peace to challenge JFK. My husband thought it would be nice to have teatime with the children and romantic dinners by ourselves. The new formula bottles lined up on the sink like tiny bombs. The U.S. was pursuing over ground testing; I was afraid the radiation would cross the milk barrier. I had a poem in me howling for real life but no language to write in. The fog came in thick, flapping about my feet like blankets unraveling. I became afraid to have a daughter.

I called Pablo Neruda in the middle of the night as he walked underwater by Isla Negra. He moved like a dream porpoise. He seemed pregnant with words. They came out of his penis in long miraculous strings. The sea creatures quivered with joy. I said, "Pablo, I want to know how to bear the child in my belly onto this bed of uranium and I want to know if a woman can be a poet." He was large as a whale. He drank the sea and spouted it in glistening odes, black and shiny. I said, "I can't have this child," and he laughed as if he had never done anything but carry and birth children.

So I packed my little bag as if I were going to the hospital and I left a note and the Wearever pots and sterilized nipples upon the glass missiles, and took the cradle board that an American Indian friend had given me for the baby and that had made my husband snort— "You're not going to carry the thing on your back, are you?" I took some money, the car, some books, paper and pens, my walking shoes, an unwieldy IBM electric typewriter, my pregnant belly and a dozen cloth diapers, and I went out.

I knew how to carry a baby and how to carry a poem and I would learn how to have a baby and even how to have a poem. I would have enough milk for both. I would learn how to walk with them. But I didn't know, and I didn't want to know, how to have a husband and a matched set of Wearever pots.

The Earth of Pablo Neruda

Pablo Neruda's cheeks arc along his jowls like the folds of old cloth. His stomach is immense. *San Pablo. San Pablo de las palabras.* I dream I am lovers with this great ugly man, am sleeping at sea level beneath the mountain of his belly, lying down on a bed of worn drawers and linen undershirts. San Pablo is the range of great hills from Chillán to Tierra del Fuego. He is the bald earth under the knife of the ice pack, the pumice fist about the fire cone of the volcano.

San Pablo Neruda wears underwear. His robe is frayed. The heavy rope belt with tassels woven of silk threads, like the one my father wore the year that I was born, rings the bells, *él pica la campana, él da una campanada de poesia.*

Pablo Neruda wears knit wool socks, a sailor's cap, and rough pants with copper buttons on the fly. His mouth bears the wide gash of a smile like the blasted entrance to Santa Maria de Iquique. His eyes have the scratch of salt. Grit of pepper under his nails, yeast smoking in his voice, skin soft as the oldest *paño de cocina.* The earth is rising in him, *como un horno de fuego* smoldering in the high desert. Bread man, potholder, *panza* of the Sierras, take me into the steaming loaf.

Exploring with Neruda

I come to Neruda the way I had pursued the great explorers when I was a child. Magellan, De Soto, Amundsen, Pizarro, Balboa compelled me with a bitter attraction. Because I am a woman, I knew that I would never be prepared for their adventures. I would never man the ship to find the undiscovered waterway, the unknown continent. But, there are ways, I insisted, through which even a woman can explore the world. I imagined an inner landscape and craved the volcanoes and high seas of the imagination. These, I believed, would display themselves to me when I found a guide to lead me to the moist stony passages between the worlds.

Neruda knew the way across. I came to Chile to follow him through an arch of granite opened by the beating of the gray turbulent sea, *el pacífico del invierno*.

When I was a very young girl, I walked the quiet blocks of my neighborhood, rounding the circle between the ocean and the bay, circling from the abandoned hospital ship, across the deserted marshes to the jetties on the farthest beaches. When I wondered why I was compelled to take this walk each night, I told myself, "I am practicing to be a poet—a poet is someone who knows how to walk."

I liked the mist, the foam and spray, salt and the slippery rocks, sand—pale as dawn—seaweed, crustaceans, silver fish, geysers and whirling undulations, mud and the obscured moon, red tides and sunrises boiling out of the sea. These were the cognates of my mind, the rise and fall, the approach and the recession, the appearance and disappearance of what I knew and did not know.

Pablo Neruda knew this territory and I came to him, not to hear his poems, nor gather his wisdom, but to follow him when he was lost, to accompany him when he was drowning, and to listen whenever he was mute. He was my Henry Hudson, the Vasco da Gama of my childhood faith. I had practiced long enough alone to want a teacher. So I followed Pablo Neruda down under the sea *a sondar* the continent of my own silence among the precipitous fathoms of the *desconocido*.

Pablo Speaks About the Girl

Once an unknown boy passed a toy sheep through a hole in a fence and I instantly became a poet. Ever since, I have been moved by the appearance of small hands, have treasured gifts and holes in fences. I walk into the fog because I never know what will be revealed when it opens its mouth. I walk into the mouth of fog as into the mouth of the shark. What is given to us, what we take, devours us. In a moment—chomp—we are holy mincemeat in the teeth of the gift.

She had small nervous hands as if she wanted to snatch away immediately what she had given. What if that little boy had been ashamed of his gift? Had thought it too small or too worn? There in the poverty of his embarrassment, a poet would have died. Don't you see, it was his clarity, his confident and unselfconscious generosity that transformed me irrevocably into the man I am.

I've been stalked before, usually by madwomen and hungry men who want to savor a bit of a poet on the installment plan. They nibble at me cautiously as if they can take a taste on consignment. If it is too bitter—spit it out.

She was neither mad nor hungry. She was painfully shy and completely unsure of herself. She could hardly speak Spanish and at times I thought English was equally difficult for her. Immediately, I knew she had the destiny to be a poet, she was so unsure of words.

I let her follow me. So respectful of my distance, she was like the wind asking permission before asserting itself upon the tree. Moments after she appeared, I forgot her, as the moving branch forgets movement, but then I remembered when her silent presence alerted me to myself. So, the branch finally knows its own stillness through its trembling. She was unsure of herself in all ways except her intractable, unshakable curiosity, except the clarity of her confident and unselfconscious right to know; finally, her curiosity determined mine.

For a girl to dare this . . . Correction, you say, at twenty-four a girl is a woman. A girl, I tell you, politics be damned, she was a girl, *una niña, nada mas,* for a girl to dare this. . . .

I wondered what she would write eventually. Oh, not about me. Such a piece, whatever it might be, would be banal. No more interesting than a seal bellying onto a rock. What would she say when she saw what she had truly come to see? I went inside myself to seek that vision for her as conscientiously as I had explored each fence hole for a secret hand.

My country was on the brink of internal war. Everything I believed in—no!— nothing I believed in, but everything I had hoped for—was about to be shattered like a wave smashed to foam against a cliff. I was old and sick—who wouldn't be? But, behind me—protecting my back from the assassin's knife of hopelessness and despair, was a girl who still believed—hoped—there was something to know.

I never walked as carefully as I did during those months when I went first and she followed. In reality, she led with her curiosity and I followed with mine as steadfastly as a gull follows a fish. I wanted to give her everything that had once mattered—the fog, the cormorants, the stones, the wet and acid earth, sand, seaweed, red tide. I gave them all to her. Soon the generals would come for everything that remained and I would die. Then, afterwards, a girl with shaking hands might have the will to shape salty mud into a world again.

The Winter of Pablo Neruda

Pablo speaks:

Soño en color. I dream in color, and awaken to the gray wave, edged white foam, playing itself free of the black sea. Gulls with bleached feathers streak across the platinum disk of the sun. My hands lose their ruddiness in the fog. I anticipate a poor meal of porridge and black olives. Someone has nicked the arteries of my country and it has gone pale; the blood of the people coagulates on the gray pavement like a black scab.

She is waiting for me in her red sweater with furry balls on both sides of her head. "Earmuffs," she whispers to me, knowing I enjoy English. The earmuffs are red. Also her nose. And her cheeks.

It will be gray in Chile this season when the spirit fades in the relentless cold, and poverty steals the blues and yellows, the ochers, greens and magentas from the eyes and heart. Or will it be fear? Or will it be despair?

In Santiago, along the Rio Mapocho, the Ramona Parra Brigada painted a long mural of stars, doves, and fists in brilliant, preposterous, primary colors now drowning in whitewash and lies. When I remember how it was, I think of all the inmates who spend their days painting the grass green. I would, myself, paint the sky blue, if I did not know that skies fall down in the black night.

I was grateful for her sweater and called to her to take my hand. It was not for love, but for the hope of the touch of the fiery red wool cuff against my wrist.

I have been given only one task in this life: not to fall into despair, and I have failed it. At least once more, I want to write something so simple, so ordinary and so familiar: "ruby lips, eyes blue as cornflowers, hair *muy negro*, porcelain hands . . ." This is not how she looks, but these commonplaces reassure me that color once existed and that I am not alone.

I asked her to model for me, to walk fast without looking back, to run without glancing over her shoulder, to leap without fear from one boulder to another. A painter might have asked her to sit without moving, but I needed the reassurance of her stride and the free song from her mouth, the pink of her tongue clanging against the rosy roof of her mouth. I wanted to see the opals of her breath in the ice crystals of frost. I had to believe that something can be alive.

Red light. Green light. *Rojo. Verde. Amarillo. Purpura. Naranja. Azul. Verde. Rojo.*

Yes, take off your clothes. Yes, I would like to see your hips move. Yes, to see your nipples redden when I pinch them.

The footprint of the soldier is always gray; it presses the color out of everything. Life freezes about the police. They bear down and we are buried under a relentless and merciless glacier.

I said nothing of this to her. I said, "Let's get a cup of tea. Tell me about your life." She was trembling. "New life," I thought, dreaming tremulous butterflies, wet and brilliant, emerging from chrysalides.

I wondered if I would love my country so much if it were not endangered. Frailty in others is an occasion for hope in oneself. The embrace is the central activity of the sea, it slides continually in erotic agitation over the limbs of the creatures it loves.

I was glad she was a woman not a child. She had a womb within her, and I was dreaming its rosy contours, its silky iridescence, its internal moiré patterns, soft and pristine. She wanted to be a poet and I was secretly betraying her, even if I wasn't planning a seduction, because I was trying to save myself by planting the seed of my imagination in her womb.

The police were going to come wanting to burn my work. The white papers still wet with black ink were threatened with foul smoke and boot prints. The air was thick with a noxious gray miasma of a lifetime come to naught. But what I might plant in her womb could grow like a secret code coming to life, a mysterious apparition, a desperate immaculate conception.

She had blood in her. She had rosy cheeks. Her lips were like rubies. Her lips were like garnets. Copper cheeks, eyes of lapis lazuli. Tongue red as an adder, fingers like salamanders, nipples like burning coals, labia sweet as peonies, anus tight as raspberries, clit like a cardinal, womb of the fire bird.

I betrayed her in the café. I wanted to make a child with her. I wanted to tell her I would die on the 23rd of September, 1973, but, if she agreed, we could have a child by the following June. She was chatting away. She was stumbling through a morass of Spanish, picking up one word then another, in no order whatsoever, but that of chance and delight. I looked at her longingly and ordered another *aguardiente*. Then I reached for her hand and told her, "Nothing . . . Nothing is more sacred than the life of a poem. It must be carried to term; it must never be aborted."

She Laments the Death of Neruda

I saw your funeral on American TV. It was a double death. The media took away what was already gone. After a few minutes, the picture shifted to Vietnam and you were erased.

I collect artifacts of the dead. The wing of an owl, the thigh bone of an elk, the heel of a buffalo, an abandoned nest sit on my altar. I would like to have, as a talisman, the three fingers that held your pen.

The last time we were together is eclipsed, like the smoke of a burning city eclipses the gun, by your death. Better that cancer had really taken you—that unnatural ravishing of the body—its peculiar and unfathomable decay as one cell after another turns against itself—than that you died of heartbreak in the middle of your own deathbed.

The last time we were together, I hoped the press of your fingers would imprint poetry upon me while I wondered how much terror I had to drink to write a poem. I felt a peculiar and unwelcome feminine reluctance to invite the world into my body.

I wanted to be one of your heirs. I wanted you to put your hand on my head the way Jacob blessed his sons and I would have gladly cheated you the way Jacob cheated Isaac into blessing him. I did not want an exclusive but I did want a portion of birthright. I wanted to know if you could imagine a woman continuing your line. Did it occur to you that a woman could carry galaxies within her womb? Do you believe the heart of a woman is large enough to carry a country, a planet, and still small enough to embrace a man and a child?

I loved you, Pablo Neruda, not the way a woman loves a man, but the way your feet loved soil, the way the moon loves death, the way you walked about Isla Negra in the rags of fog, the way the sun hankers for the green rush in all living things, and the way the mouth hungers for a word. And I still love you, Pablo Neruda, and want to snatch the white birdsong from your beak as you streak across the white sky in your white plumage cawing at the birds of death.

Burying Our Dead, Pablo Neruda

Santiago, Chile, December 12. 1992, [UPI]. The Chilean government said Tuesday it would exhume the body of Nobel Prize-winning poet Pablo Neruda and re-inter his remains on the island of Isla Negra in accordance with his wishes.

The famous writer died 10 days after General Augusto Pinochet took power in a 1973 military coup during which the country's president and Neruda's close friend, Salvador Allende, died.

Pinochet had refused to allow Neruda's remains on Isla Negra as the poet had expressed in his poem, "Canto General."

This Pablo, is the story.

It began with a *poncho*. I bought it in Peru on the way to Chile. This morning I wanted its warmth, the comfort of the weave, the dark red bloodlines. It had been put away with part of my life.

This morning, I thought, winter is coming, I must wear red. I was prepared. I put on the red cowboy boots I had bought second hand from a woman in Texas and I borrowed a red wool scarf from a friend in Chicago. I had imagined red earmuffs, Pablo, when I had also imagined that I was following you alongside the gray icy sea surrounding Isla Negra. Red surrounds me again. Blood and sun, Pablo, in the graying winter of despair.

This morning, I found the *poncho* in the bottom of the wooden chest among cedar blocks and mothballs. When I put it on, I was a girl again. I could speak Spanish once more. My heart opened and a stream of doves, *amor y palomas*, flew out along beams of ruby light as if we were celebrating a birthday.

This evening, I heard the news on the radio. They are going to dig up your bones, Pablo Neruda. They will dig up your bones with the care given to an archaeological treasure. They will remove the grasses and snails by your feet, your lovers like flags over your swaying cock, *las sopas y los vinos tintos* on the roof of your belly, the poor and *las putas* on your heart, your poems like seed pearls across your throat, Chile engraved on your forehead, *y un espuma d'esperanza*, a spume of hope, the clouds of the spouting sea, gushing from the dome *de su cabeza*, raising your blue cap, *azul, azul, azul*, in a greeting which opens the eyes of the comely figureheads on all the drowned ships in the depths around Isla Negra.

They will find a place for each knuckle, each rib, each femur and vertebra, for *los huesos* of ivory and moonstone. The bones of the hand and the bones of the feet. The elbows, the knees and the jaw. They will make a man of your bones, Pablo Neruda, and lay him out in the black rocky soil as the red sun sets, the winter sea afire in the *sanctuario de sangre* that is Isla Negra.

It began with a *poncho*, Pablo Neruda, and it ends with a *poncho*, Pablo Neruda. A *poncho* I bought in Cuzco below the sacred mountain and it led me to Chile where I lived for some weeks in the wind that you were also breathing. There was a time when we lived in the same ruddy air.

So breathe, Pablo Neruda. Now, breathe, once more. Breathe in the sand and the wind and the sea. Breathe in the elements and breathe out fire, Pablo Neruda. We cover the grave, Pablo Neruda, and stand on your body, a holy volcano rising from the carmine waters. Give us the beginning and the end, the red seas, the whirlpools and the geysers, the rain of wine and embers, the bloodstones, the fire opals and the red mantle, Pablo Neruda.

We will also be born and die. Give us the right piece of earth, the right wool, the right dyes and the loom to transform a red *poncho* into a shroud. Hold us, Pablo Neruda, in the wool and the weave as we descend and we rise.

And sing:

Rojo y rojo y rojo
rojo y rojo.

Hidden Light

In the moment of trying to understand, the light comes. Not only the light, but the light beneath the light. If I had not looked up from my own confusion, I would have missed the two deer walking soundlessly across the smallest meadow. Now, here come the turkeys, including the one with the brownest feathers who listens and is most apart.

This time Old Man Turkey has come with his harem. He has alert and observant eyes and an intelligent face poking out of his red and white woven *kafiyah* and a silky black beard, knotted and shining as the tassels on a holy *tallit*. He moves, camel-like, as they do too, his beloveds, nodding his head, looking down, nodding his head. So I assume as I find myself among these gleaners, that he, and they, also, are praying.

When I awakened this morning, there was a stole of fog across the shoulders of the mountain and the thinnest sheen of frost dimming the glass. What was behind all that whiteness, I couldn't see. Yet now the light that is under light appears.

This is the mystery. It had been raining and so I was indoors. But the turkeys came and I heard them muttering to themselves as they sometimes do when searching for corn and seeds. If I hadn't heard them davening, if I hadn't imagined they were calling to me in a language we both know, I wouldn't have seen the faintest beginning, almost imperceptible, of a rainbow.

They called and I went out. The rainbow darkened. That is, it brightened. Light cannot be separate from its dark. The indigo deepened and expanded until it was itself the width of the rainbow. There was rainbow and there was dark and the two together making an arc across the grove of trees that mark the boundary of the smallest meadow. Then the indigo birthed from its side, as from a rib, another rainbow. Now the arc was radiant and dark and radiant again against the indigo darkness from which the rain fell gladly.

Would that not have been sufficient for a lifetime of praise?

As I stood there peering into the darkness and what can emerge from it, the trees at the edge of the grove, just footsteps away, were gilded with the brilliance of sunlight, a small circle of light, the size of a sun. Not only the rainbow, but the making of the rainbow was before me.

They say there is a pot of gold at the end of the rainbow, but here in this moment, the gold was raining down. That is why I said the rain fell gladly. I ran toward it, my arms outstretched, I wanted to be bathed in it, in rain and color and light, all of it. But, it withdrew to where I could not reach it. I fell back to where I had been standing when it first appeared before me. There is something else that could be said about the presence of such a rainbow, but I do not dare.

In the wet grass that gleamed wherever it was touched by light, lay two iridescent turkey underfeathers. Rainbow feathers. Such a gift. As if I might someday need to be reminded that I had been in the presence of the light within the light.

Lights Like Stars

Lights like stars, we say,
who have never been to a star,
and so cannot imagine such light
though we persist in believing
an instrument, flying by,
can measure light,
and tell us
everything we need to know.

Might There Be a Thousand Words for Light

The shadow lands
emerge, a geography
establishes itself out of mist.
We wish to participate in creation
but we are just a flicker,
a wink of an electron
in the vast light field of eternity,
and yet for us, it is a lifetime,
sufficient, for a tower to rise
and to fall.

As many words
the Inuit have for snow,
I want for light. The way
the rain falls and the light
penetrates each drop,
or the shimmer
of a single bead of water
configuring itself into
the original complexity of snow,
and then that light
descending in the disguise of white.

The towers fell and
continue falling. Years later
they haven't ceased falling. Rubble
to rubble, a lateral avalanche
bringing everything down.
Anguished and impotent
against the new skies falling,
we wreak the ancient images
making debris
out of the oldest beauty.

We thought the purpose
was birth, but what
if it has become destruction?
What if we are to raze
everything to the ground
in the last sweep of the hand
on the way to oblivion. If so,

the great war lord
is an obedient servant
of emptiness.

What if everything that we raised
is to be razed, so that our souls
can be born again into the empty field
that is only grass,
with cows and calves,
elk, elephants, goats, whales
waiting at the perimeter
for a ceremony of welcoming.

It is early afternoon
and the green is becoming itself
against the gray of rain.
Venus is a boiling planet
that has lost all mist and cataract.
It could happen here,
water fleeing
because she does not
want to be a war.

How careful we must be
with rubble,
to return each particle
to the original cell.
The minute gathers the minute,
a single drop of water
gathers single drops of water,
photon by photon.
The thousand words for light
descend
into the dissolution.

Here comes the green,
its own covenant,
and the cows, openmouthed,
teaching the calves the way
of grinding down to the core.
Hope is a great muddy delta
emerging out of the mouth
of water.

What have we not spoken of?
What have we forgotten?
The wind. The firestorm.
The tornado. Thunder beings
strike lightning into the heart
and scar the brow. Afterwards,
the chief of birds can see
through the dark that the moon
casts over all things.

Here come the shadow lands,
and not a living thing
except the blessed cows
devouring what the light and water
bring forth when we are still.

Moon Song

The mockingbird will sing all night
along the violin string of the moon rising,
or the moon will rise
up the ladder of birdsong until dawn.
The dark knows this;
it enfolds these lovers
in the serenity of its many arms.

Fires

In my childhood fevers,
the light that mattered
came from a dark place.
My dreams were blazing with it
before the three houses on the Boardwalk
and then Luna Park burned down,
before I watched the fireworks
each Tuesday summer night,
She stood,
carrying herself like a torch
at the foot of my bed
in a rain of meteors.

When I could walk alone,
when the days were short,
I followed the lighthouse. Later,
the nights were full of fireflies.
My sons caught them
in a mason jar;
it was our lantern.
We went north one summer
where the sun set near midnight.
We took in the light,
drank it like water;
it muddied our hands.

The last time I saw her,
the woman in the small box
was luminous,
then we buried her.

Sun

Sun
blazes through
the feathers
of the bird in flight.
What could obscure,
carries light.

Hawk

Hawk,
  circling,
  carrying light
  on her back.
  The turning letters,
  hungry for Creation.

Sometimes in Concert with the Gods

The sun going down resembled a moon.
Only the faintest scar of gray
crossed the yellow disk.
Heifetz, in the bowl of Turkish mountains,
playing to the nightingales,
was answered, song for song.
Memories are the miner's light,
the yellow birds carry
into the dark shaft
to keep us safe.
The sun fell into the blue mountain,
the mountain opened and swallowed the sun,
yellow as the rising moon.

At eight, in a fever,
I dreamed a stairway of light,
yellow rabbits on my bed, and God.
Steam in the black iron pot
on the gas flames,
cobalt blue and cadmium yellow,
ochre, saffron, lemon, xanthous, chrome.

At the end of the street,
beyond the gatehouse
and the barbed wire,
and before the black breakwater,
was the lighthouse;
we were never without light.
We lived on a point of land,
a sandy sliver
jutting into the dark straits.
Memories streaking down my back
in yellow chalk.

The first day,
the acacia was a light in the room,
but then it dried.
Its insistent yellow,
from a distance, seemed the same,

153

but, standing next to the tree,
I saw the light inside was gone.
The day after she died,
the tree fell down.

At Sounion, the sea
put on the clothes of the sun,
was all gold and amber,
was light itself.
Then the sun vanished,
the sea had eaten it
for the dark.
Last birds flew over
in a blue sweep, singing.
Poseidon had been there
for thousands of years
and his temple fallen down.

Walking the Creek

Waters from the snowy, sacred mountain,
place of perfect balance, say the Chumash,
once seeped down into the creek all year, cold
even in August's fire season,
and then afterwards, into September
even until the first rains of Thanksgiving,
a trickle of the old stream flowed.

Walking the creek this July morning,
dusty river stones mark the graves
of reeds alongside corpses of trees,
the brown dust of dry leaves,
this year's season, amber on the ground
where we have known loam.

I dreamed Fire, in all her raiment,
came over the ridge, and a petitioner
took his drum and began praying
as if on his knees,
Praise to the Great One, as She descended
among the torches of great oaks
and the fireworks of pines.

Fire is a god,
the hidden one, her power
contained in stars,
the nuclei of strange particles and
the sacred magma at the core of planet earth.
We cannot drink it,
we must not take it in our hands,
it does not serve us
to breathe it in.

> Michael, the Archangel, Water,
> and Gabriel, the Archangel, Fire,
> together they are the peacemakers
> who form heaven, *Sh'mayim*,
> through the gathering
> of the holy letters,
> *Shin*, the eternal flame,
> *Esh* at the core of fire,

and *Mem*, the essence
of the sacred water, *Mayim*,
Sh'mayim, heaven,
includes *Yud*, the Divine itself,
and *Aleph*, the silent one,
at the beginning of beginnings,
ever present in the word.

Fire season, we call it,
not knowing, not wanting to know
the Holy One. Instead we make
a furnace of our world,
separating the sacred from the sacred,
water from fire,
splitting the atom of paradise,
fulfilling the prophecy of ultimate sin
written this century
in the burning bodies of holocausts,
and the oldest ancestor's oily bodies.
The world is no longer
the Temple of the Sacred:

Therefore, isn't it a sacrilege to call for Rain?

What the Trees Know

It is hot and still.
Thunderclouds moving,
unmoving.
The leaves and grasses
flutter slightly only
when I pray for the song
the trees want to hear us
sing to make amends.

Everywhere I look,
everywhere, there are stumps.
The trees are aware, always,
of their kin cut down.
These deaths are different
from falling, falling
and rising up again,
even from the same body.

How the men go on
about the bear, deer and elephants
destroying the trees and woodlands.
But in the lifetime of trees,
that can be hundreds
or thousands of years,
no ultimate harm comes
from how they live.
They have worked it out together.
This is what we do not understand:
Together. Together,
a word we do not know.

And so the clouds pass us by
again. And the heat settles
into a slow burn
as smoke rises somewhere.
in the western sky,
The sun has turned from white
to magenta, and the bandit moon
has a red bandana across her mouth.
And even if, as legend says,
the trees hold water in their roots

for each other and
this keeps the soil
from burning everywhere,
it is so hot
they will flame soon.

Regardless, the night
will not come to ease us.

The Bird in the Heart of the Tree

Seeing the movement down the tree, the descent of spirit into matter, or a singing bird, with blue feathers leaping from branch to branch.

Spirit breaks into song, breaks itself into pieces to sing, a part of what is indivisible enters the universe in a body, a feather, a color or a note.

Spirit entering into form, breaks off from itself, breaks itself, breaks itself into pieces, is broken. Wherever we see spirit, there is something broken.

Here the heart is broken, here the spirit enters. The prayers of a broken heart call the spirit in, are therefore whole.

The song enters the world. Here, there is someone singing. A different melody, exactly the same, is coming from farther away than time. The two songs meet in a corner of the garden, in the very heart of the tree. *Tepheret* is the place of their meeting.

Tepheret is the place where the prayer is spoken. Or it is the place where the prayer is heard. Is the meeting place.

The bird is always praying. Even when it is asleep, the song is alive in it. The heart of the bird is a small drum, and the drum is beating out its song. When the dawn comes, the melody is awakened by the light. Or if it is a nightbird, it sings all night long.

The song is never lonely, but the bird is longing for the song. In the moment of song, there is prayer, or in the moment of prayer there is song. Everything has a home.

Every prayer is answered. The bird in exile sending a message to the song or asking for the dawn to break. In the moment of prayer, exile disappears. When we are praying, we have come home.

When I pray, I do not know whether I am climbing a tree or making a ladder for the light to climb down. Whether I am calling the bird to my hand or flying to meet it among the leaves

Sometimes the bird turns away. Sometimes it does not open its mouth to sing. Sometimes it is afraid. Sometimes it is afraid of the dark. But when it forgets fear and opens its mouth to sing, it fills with light.

There was a place where we expected the birds to disappear. But because the heart was broken, the prayers existed. No matter how heavy the earth, the air can always bear the song of birds.

The light of prayer travels faster than the speed of light. It takes no time for the light of prayer to travel between the worlds. So even in that place, prayer existed, and reached its destination. Even in that place. And even in that place, there are birdsongs still.

Prayer exits, light enters us, anywhere. Prayer is the call and the light is the answer. The bird calls and the song appears. Sometimes the birds sing so sweetly, the tree itself is made of light. Day and night. Inseparable. Indistinguishable.

There is a hollow in the heart of a tree that was pecked out by the bill of a singing bird. Who knows the grief the tree felt with the incessant pecking.

Sometimes gratitude, sometimes praise. Sometimes longing. A night owl on the one tree calling to another night owl in its branches.

A song without beginning and without end, breaking into notes, a light breaking into colors. All the pain of breaking. The beauty of it. The pain and the beauty. Beauty is the very heart of it. With all its brokenness, beauty is the heart of it.

In the Garden there is a Tree. And in the Tree is a Bird, a Bird with blue feathers. It sits in a nest it has carved into the very heart of the Tree. The Bird is singing. It is singing so sweetly, the Tree fills with Light.

A Song emerges from the Nest of Light in the Great Heart of the Tree. *Tepheret*. The Tree is full of Birds. Each Bird is full of Light. And the Light, it, is also Singing.

Gathering at the Gates

Moonshine

"I have heard it before," Barbara says, disappointed that after twenty years she should be picking up a poem to find the same dilemma unsolved. The moon is milky. We walk out of the house to say good-bye. "We take lovers," I tell her, "to remember the sky." She is not pleased that after twenty years, I have not learned there is something fresher in the wind. Above us the invaded and defeated moon glows with eerie light, the white heat of its pulse eats against my skin and pulls on the white geyser in the body. "It's the same milk cry," I say. "You've said that before," she says, "and the theme of milk boiling in you has been there for twenty years." We've talked about this liquid that is the oil of us, the riches in us, but though my fingers reach to it, I have not gotten closer. What the fingers strive to clutch remains stubbornly ungraspable beneath the skin.

"I have heard this before," Barbara says, and yet I am not through with it this evening of the milky sky when the white haze reminds me that tomorrow, the miracle, obvious and constant as the morning paper, will still elude me as I squint to read the headlines, taking in the airplane crashes, fires, shooting deaths and oil spills; and the men upon the moon no nearer to the white oil than I am.

In the morning, I will need to know again how it is the world turns and remains on the same point, the principles of rotation and revolution which I remember from high school science, and that the moon turns twice also but along an egg following the sun. We stand on point like a dancer lost in the moment, the little dolls on Broadway that sailors buy, the music box devoted to the perpetual ballerina, if there are still sailors like the ones I found on the subway and brought home. Or are they now the adventurers who sweep in from the white Alaska pipeline, thin, acned, scared and full of small bills and coins in their pockets, looking to sleep on water beds and rock with the lunar tide or to bend in the broken curve of old mattresses after being fed on the same sandwiches of rye bread and leftover roast? And what do they have to do with milk those who pass the black tar across the tundra, casting the same shadows on the snow that the man casts who steps with his boots upon the moon?

Twenty-five years after the sailors, there is the same ache and the same illusive sweat upon the skin, the same nerves, the same certainty in my body that there is something to be known which I have not come to know. There was the sailor who climbed into my car at a red light, pressing a knife to my ribs in the daytime when the moon hid long enough for me to drive into a gas station—SUNOCO—so he got out casually grinning moonily, "Thanks for the ride, baby." Something to be gotten at remains elusive as those sailors whose names I don't remember, coming from the Broadway dark into my house to be fed bread cut with a butcher knife.

To be adolescent again, reduced in my womanhood to the same awkward teenager as ignorant as my own small sons and to continue to poke in a brazen manner, index finger, thumb, blade, into the places that yield. And coming to the smell of it, more odor than the aftertaste of goat in the milk, and a new love growing in me swelling crescents, fourteen days to turn and fourteen days back. And it's time to milk the cows again, they bleat with the fullness in their udders, but the city girl can't pull it out fast enough. She doesn't have the muscle or the rhythm to milk the teats dry, and there's something in the formula of milk she doesn't understand as she sits there talking to the cows, listening to the incomprehensible mooing. It's in your body and in mine, something I haven't found yet and no one seems to know or care though some advise moon ships and rocket probes to find new images, but this sticks like an old skin of milk.

"Why is it," she asks, "it is with a man that you look at the moon?" I repeat, "It is why we take lovers." A friend said we could control our bodies by sleeping in an absolutely dark room, black silk sheets over the windows. Open the window once during the month and turn your skin to the moonlight and the egg will push out toward it and wait its three days, waxing and waning, before it drops away. In those nights of moonlight, you must not sleep with a man unless you want a child.

So the old images persist as the moon reappears. Neither the twenty years of poems nor the landing ships and scientific instruments from Texas have exhausted this old obsession or revealed anything, but that something lies beneath the surfaces we raze with metal scoops to find metals or some white oil to keep the heat burning. The blunt miracle of cheese persisting while we sit around the pool with our chests naked to the sun, the ordinary genitals turning slightly pink. Despite our casual demeanor, I do not tell you about the sailors I brought home or the soldiers that I danced with in army camps, because, as I said then, "They are lonely and there is no war on." Was it because they didn't speak any language I knew that we danced and looked up at the moon and the man in it and said good-bye with sweaty palms and bellies full of legal moonshine. And I wonder about the men who go off to build the pipelines in Alaska and attack caribou that graze upon the moon. And what does the astronaut launched in Florida and controlled in Texas think as his spaceship scratches the moon dust and what does he learn with his crude metallic instruments that probe the dark side?

And I confess a turning point: In the park learning the Tai Chi forms which are the black and white crescents of the moon, the Guernsey cow, I found another soldier who asked if he could learn the rhythms too. "I am a mercenary," he said, "and round in my motions." I didn't take out my little Swiss army knife and stab delicate half circles between his ribs. I didn't ask him who he killed, which of my sisters or brothers he had dropped fire on, which of the people the sun burns dark, he had darkened further, but said he could learn the moon dance, thinking it might burn into him, white as napalm, as he had burned death into others and then the larger blade in his hand might drop.

Something from the dark teases me as you walk toward me from a nightmare the first night we spend together, the moon coming over our bodies and the trees playing animal shapes against the light. You wake afraid that I will tear your common secret from you without knowing that it has been twenty-seven years I have been looking for it, and it still waves at me like a sailor saying he is going back to the ship when I know the man entering the subway is only retreating to Broadway and to the little dolls which twirl, to the music boxes, the post cards, the women who know how to wear black stockings and white shoes, and to the boys whose pants are even tighter than mine across the ass. I also learned the fashion of the street, wore boots with little moon-shaped heels, sharp as scimitars, and leather belts tight about my waist, and pushed up my breasts over crescents of wire so that they looked like plump moons.

But with all the instruments created for exploration, something eludes me, and maybe it is because in the last instant after the sheets open to the moonlight, I don't dare be anything but polite. Lying down, clean and ready for the body, which approaches me with familiar passion, knowing each time there is something I don't dare, ignorant of how to dare it.

Knowing now that the moon has no voices, that it is quieter than I thought and not to be gotten at with a knife as I had imagined, fantasizing, and not daring, the switchblade in my own hand, used against my own self, ripping my own body open so someone can enter. "I've heard this before," Barbara says. "Yes," I answer, "but this time it's different; see where we are in the orbit."

Do you remember, Barbara, the man in New York who passed us wearing a little silver razor blade about his neck? Later you learned it was for cocaine, white moon powder, but I thought it was for violence and still believe I'm right. Remember the little pocket knives flicked into the dirt as we played marbles, trading hard swirling moons and carrying them home clicking, blue white and moonstone against the steel blades and coming in thirsty for a cold glass of milk? "I've heard all this before," Barbara repeats, but listens while I go off looking, because I can hear, without seeing, the voices in the bushes teasing, "You're hot; you're cold," like the two sides of the moon.

I remember that yesterday we drove across the city and I saw the moon red and fat and close as a belly and I said, "Look, look at the moon." But there was something in the way of your seeing it. The moon was playing hide and seek with us behind buildings and I said, "Let's go to the top of the hill so you can see it," and agreeing you drove straight on saying you had seen the moon before. And suddenly it didn't matter, we had both seen the moon before and it would return faithful to its fourteen days of coming and going.

"I want to understand the body." "You always do," she says, "when you're in love. You think the body can catch something and hold it like it catches a child." The moon is quiet. There is no air. You cannot talk there. When we get there it's hot or cold, and the light or dark we chase hovers through the dust we kick up with our big metal feet. We are mute and dumb there and look aside while the common secret balances just out of reach. And having used a knife before, I turn aside from it without scorn for those who wield it, knowing what desperation brings them to cut, stab, slash, a knife going into the broken mattress looking for coins and green bills, while the bird feathers fly in a white haze about the room. It isn't there. It isn't with a knife that we find it, but there is a common secret just beyond the sperm and orgasm, or just before it, a simple coupling like the light of the sun upon the moon. I can't ignore the man in the moon or the shadow of black and white.

The moon never stops turning, and we turn with it, a dancer on point, we travel that ellipse around the sun and the first hint of the moon, like a little trickle of white thin milk, slips across the sky as we sit under an apricot tree. You cut a fruit into half circles and there's the bleat of the goat around us, only it is just a dog barking, and the next door neighbors making love in front of the blue glow of the television set, and while there is still something I want to know, it's fading as the sun and moon angle from each other.

And I may have to wait another month to know the common secret, to end the mystery once and for all by entering it through the early dark places, the ordinary doorways, where the sailors disappear. Or by standing silently under the constant moon which sees the dark earth coming and knows what turns in that turning.

Nuptuals

That afternoon,
knee deep in leaves
before the autumn burning,
scattering what ripens,
what falls, what dies,
we traced
the secret ribs and veins
rising with the water in the tree,
until our holy vows
were in the sky,
the clouds,
also drifting, orange,
everything flaming.

Then loss was not age,
was not the leaf song
under our feet,
We were the new hearth fire.
Still, we were pulled apart,
even as branches
set out
in the four directions.

We were six,
at that wedding of children,
we were saplings,
we were the morning,
we were the morning star.

Now, I want something else
from the tree,
not innocence,
but perfect knowledge
knee deep in leaves,
while bending
toward holy matrimony
in the beginning of each year.

The Mystery of the Birds

In the morning we were seated in the garden
learning the way.

The mystery in ecstatic feathers,
crimson, lapis, amber, vermilion,
is enamored with the dusky gray bird.
The male desires the invisible
while she must be satisfied with splendor.

The sap is running evenly
up and down
the World Tree.
In a universe without direction,
the center is everywhere.

Last night, after a season
of a single tone,
an owl answered another lonely owl
and then, unable to keep
their calls separate,
they mated

in separate octaves of song
before ten women in a room
on the eve of a wedding.

This is the secret:
great striped and speckled creatures
feel rapture in the presence of the plain.

Here is the practice:
      Behold!
           Be aware
                 Touch
                       Bow down in awe.

That Woman Is Talking to Herself

Lost this morning
in the gale,
as the rain is lost in it.
I know this wind
with my eyes closed.
These fingers wizened
with the alphabet of the deaf
grasp at the invisible,
while I go forth
only with a faith in rope.
Things held in place,
the gods pulling on us,
at each hand,
the tether is
the morning star.

My elbows say,
brace yourself in ribs
while the feet
of the universe
run from each other.
Going abroad,
I hunt the streets
of the moon,
bemoaning the only voice,
wind,
and the duet in my throat.

Everywhere, the gods
speaking through holes
in my coat.

Desertion

What covers me
in this wilderness
is the rope of night,
this tent of skin.
I surround myself
with nomads,
guides who know the desert
and are lost as well.
They make
a god
of it.

My father is
one of ten tribes
called Wandering,
when there was
nothing,
he named it
One.

In this harsh place,
I touch my lips for salt,
there is no water,
we are reduced
in all things,
until there is nothing
to honor
but the foot.
Still, I believe in goats
and do not close
my eyes
to the emptiness,
though I am given nothing
but horizons.

Here, I paint dreams
on the sand,
healing the cracks
in my fingers,
while the wind
calls upon the gods
to speak to me
without pity.

The Open Hand

At the whisper of the Presence, we open our palms
to see the life inscribed.
The rain is not sufficient and the dolphins are beaching themselves,
while stones in the far distant sky are singing to us, and

the asters we pick in the field have been imagined by stars.
First, the moonlight brightened and blinded us
and then the shadow fell on it and we were blind in the dark.
We imagined goodness, but we didn't know it would weary us so.

The hand of God is a cloudy field upon our heads,
is the silence of a great light.
The only way we know that we are close enough
is when everything below disappears.

After you finally connect one thing to another,
you learn what was ripped apart before you were born.
The breast that was cut off from my body
is a fountain of milk running downstream,

the legs that were taken from you
are another river that washes us clean.
You always say what is entirely unexpected,
requiring us to live according to what cannot be known.

When one has the gift of turning one thing into another,
he finds a cave and works in the dark.
I see that you have been given the task of naming,
of saying those words you have been given to say:

The Place, the Name, the One
        The Holy Place, the Holy Name, the Holy One.

A Tree That Has Not Fallen

For Victor

The roots of all living things are tied together.
When a mighty tree is felled, a star falls from the sky . . .
—Chan K'in of Naha

A tree—it has not fallen—
held to a star in the sky.
A light,
beneath your feet,
Chan K'in, the old one,
tethers you to this life,

while the words rush together—
confusion, dissolution, purification—
to renew
in the alchemical vessel,
your heart.

We sit beside you,
the palms of your hands
soft as age,
then walk up the muddy path
to the top of the hill
where you exclaim most clearly,
"Look, it is like a jungle."

Alongside you now,
as it has always been,
we go as far as we can,
then wait for your return
from the underbrush of knowing
from the worlds
you have always dared to explore,
alone.

Return to Earth[14]

You know how to track,
we walk in the dark,
two rabbits across
the snow, one with
great leaping feet.

I want your birthright,
I say you have to take
what belongs to the old man.
I will also put on fur,
extend a hairy arm
to get what would have gone
to a brother.

Every day, I visit
the great, twisted
tree, her arms
not lowered by the snow.

To have a life,
even a woman must
stake her claim
on the land, otherwise
we only have
what we shared,
the sweet and bitter
berry thorns,
dying in my room
this entire month.

---

14   We are each / the only world / we are going to get. —Jim Harrison, "Return to Earth"

Stands Across the Frigid Moon[15]

I gave you
what I had,
everything soft,
literate and informed
by the heart.
I thought it
was sufficient
to offer you
what had entitled me.

One grandfather left
the farm. He had only had a cow,
his life quiet
as a barn.
The other worked
in wood,
a carpenter is
an honest man.

Now in this winter
country, still
too polite,
I offer you
rocks, gale,
the bare scraped
earth, temperatures
20 below and
the white
terrible snow.

We do not know
the name of our blood

—Gypsy,
      Indian,
      bleak hunting moon
      give me a
      sign.
      Silver
      protect you
      as you climb.

---

15   Title from "Before Completion," in *Palmistry for Blind Mariners*, by Judith Minty.

The steppe is
in your eye, barbarian
hordes, harsh granite
in our bones,
you do not need
a will
to want the land.

Become One with Me

A silence grows somewhere about my heart. It is the silence between all the words. It enters the way lovers are surprised by each body vanishing in the other.

I open my mouth. Breath enters, filling the loneliness. When I die, I will remain part of the earth. There is no way to escape the bond. Even a capsule with dead men will not circle the earth endlessly. They will be pulled down to the soil. I could not pull away from the earth if that were necessary to save it.

In a poor country, my friend sits with his wife, the pistol they share upon his lap. The small man with a limp used to be a dancer. The bombs from my country are falling nearby, silver as rain. Alongside beans and coffee, he is growing orchids. What would you like me to say?

This silence when the words are falling away. Also, I do not know if I can manage the larger silence that they say saves something.

Finches mating in our wedding baskets under the eaves. The one with the red throat flutters on the back of the downy one. A seed is passed from beak to beak. A twig in the mouth or a bit of fur. Long, fine silk hairs braided into the chalky scat on the trail. Sometimes a bobcat prowls by my window toward the hills. Flowers, still wild, small and scattered like snow.

From out of a mire of leaves on the copper of madrone laurel, the triumphant sprint of a single flowering peach twig announces itself. I spend the day releasing it from the confinement of passionate branches wondering: Do I have the right to strike down the wild thing for the domestic fruit?

A woman in a blue Chevy parked at the edge of the fragrant sage speaks: "I play God," she says to no one at all, "and God plays the chord." There is the sound of a wooden flute, I think.

Madrone poisons me with its touch. Sap insists itself under my skin, wants me to carry it. I can only bemoan the body that flares at the necessary intermingling of species. This penetration burns. There is nothing to be done but to cover myself with clay, to bury myself in earth.

"Neither hot nor cold can pass this point," says the sutra. Nothing that is only itself can pass over the river. Anything that is so completely itself, is partial, is only itself, is not another, is a broken thing, is fractioned, is only a fragment, is like the flower that the bomb has exploded. Anything that is completely itself can never be whole.

There is something in a word. I can hear it now. Something other than the ordering of one word after another, something other than the meaning or the song, something else. Something in the word itself. Or rather, when it sits next to another word, something is there, two lovers on a bench, that secret. The words open their musk and the net is visible. Everything is caught.

The war thinks it can be one by itself. The war thinks it can be won by itself. The war cuts itself into pieces. It whittles itself down. When we all disappear, it will be so much itself, it will be so large, there will be nothing left of it. Without me, the war is only a splinter and that, itself, broken. The war will remain by itself, like a dry husk, on the disappearing side of the dry river.

Each spring for seven years now, the owls call to each other all night in slow and leisurely conversations. Suddenly, I hear a rapid trill of two voices at once. I bless their mating in the dark, the quick duet. And now they're singing again, in the time it takes to formulate the question and then the answer.

I am saying the name of my friend. I am saying it again and again. I am saying it like a rosary or a cord of amber beads, or a mantra of jade, or the fringe on a *tallit*, or a necklace of turquoise and silver, or a prayer wheel loose in the wind. I am turning the hour and the day and the year on the axis of his name. I am watching the earth spin on the point of the sacred alphabet of his name. I am spinning the bombs away. I am spinning them faster than light. I am spinning the silver of bombs into a thread of light that cannot disappear us. As long as I remember my friend, he will stay alive.

So I marry you again and again. I want to become one with you. I can hear the silence in the silence coming like a wild storm. It is falling upon us. The world is a great knot and we are tied into it, one into the other. Here the word is singing itself into being on this other side of the living waters of the river.

Einstein, the Lighthouse

Climbing the backbone of time,
you saw light propelled like a knife,
a thin gash streaking across the sky,
and imagined glowing rings,
incandescent fragrance of the stars,
not the terrible fire of fires,
not the Milky Way drawn and quartered
by the saddled horses of the apocalypse,
that crucifixion of algebra geometry,
not the war that will end all,
the wasteland without suns or moons.

Divine kindness
calls one electron to another,
despite the expanding space in the universe
is the ether of the tenderness of the Great Mother
holding the galaxies together in a milky light.
Einstein, the lighthouse,
is the flames without flames budding
on the world tree,
a carpet of chrysanthemums
from here to infinity
for the feet of the White Lady
who forgives all,
the silence of fireflies,
meadows and galaxies asleep
in past and future snows.

Water Falling in the Late Afternoon

I had to be a certain age before I could tell this the way it was shown to me, the discovery of a hidden spring in the dry season. I was at the age when the grief of having lost everything awakened me to water gushing mysteriously out of the very heart of clay, creating a flood of vines clambering the oaks and climbing toward the meadow of sagebrush while singing with the exotic imaginings of mosquitoes.

The difficulty of finding craft after one has been away a long time. Memory remaining in the hands, but gone from the mind, as if the wind had come up without the bell being struck. And when it returns, it is, at first, only a faint stirring, as is inevitable when the sun sinks and the dark places cool.

In truth, I had been lost for such a long time that I had forgotten water and its source. Even sitting beside it I still forgot, except in the course of the day, the sunlight occasionally lifted shadow out of the leaves with the coming or going of the breeze and intermittent and accidental moments of beauty skittered through the dappled light. The water rushed past me swollen with the rain that had fallen months ago until finally, I could say beauty knowing how fleeting it is, or how abundant.

Then like the breeze, again, the young girl whom I would have called Morning if I had been chosen to name her, stuck a shovel in the twilight earth and with another hand held back the flagrant abundance of lilies, irises, bearded and black, moon-faced roses beaming with strange pink dust as of rose quartz rubbed milky in the river. And with the same audacity, the girl found another entrance for a pot of blue stars that would curl closed in the coming moonlight as if bending about water.

The girl laughed, delighted, of course, in being admired or seen for what she is. The beauty that was all around us in the night coming in on a rush of stars, light falling into the clarity of blue, darkening, waterfalls of night and grief, streaming toward us.

The young girl, laughing, bronze, holding the morning in her own light, and the vigor of the shovel insistent in the earth, planted the blue flowers, which she called *Felicidades*, as if she really knew the name for joy and would hold it as the blue light came running fast and breathless toward us, her laughter cascading down the rocky streambed of the vanishing afternoon.

The blessing of the turning of the axis so that the shape of darkness follows in the curve of the silhouette of light. And endlessly so. The sunset and the moonrise. The stars, black night, sinking into the sea just as the sun rises from the water. Thus the sunlight and the night breaking blue and endless cataracts of water falling about us.

Naming Us by Our Eyes

A Remembrance of Charlie Chaplin for Ariel

In the beginning we walk on the beach or it is raining or both and the mist may be the spray of the ocean but it is the end of a drought and I am grateful for the rain like the time it was raining in Santiago when we met. And what we are trying to accomplish now is a sunburst and you stand at the water's edge and I walk toward you across the sand and a man stops me. He says, "The sun hasn't come out though I prayed for it." "Don't pray now," I beg him, "it's after sunset. I've had enough miracles today." You're on the beach and we're together and the drought is over. Last night your plane was twelve hours late but the CIA didn't get you and you said you had no trouble with immigration and you're here and the sea hovers about us; that is miracle enough. The man says, "It doesn't matter." He'll pray tomorrow. "There's a sun," he says. He knows that for sure. He's seen it though not since you've come. He says he swears it exists. He knows that for a fact.

In the beginning we walk on the California beach and you say it is your ocean like the one in Chile, a little wild and gray and powerful. And you say you'll take me there when the Junta's dead and we think next year is a good year, even this year. We're ready. And we look at the sea and I think it's not only where we're coming from but where we're going.

I put my feet in the water and know that something of me will eventually be carried down to Chile and we can send messages in bottles to those who have remained there. The fish will transport what we wish. The Junta cannot defeat what the ocean carries though they would, if they could, pass a law against the sea, knowing that it holds us. Ultimately they are defeated in every corner. I look at the sea wondering if it is a woman. *La Mer*. Or a man. *El Mar*. Or is it one of those new androgynous creatures we aspire to be? Man and woman in our hearts. We walk on the beach and you say "Someday we will all be entirely woman." But in your poem you said entirely human. *Enteramente humanos*. I think we will all be entirely each other and then we will be ourselves. The ocean leaps toward us with its undefeatable arms.

We are walking the beach, the sun has fallen behind the rain into the sea and steams the air sweet with fish. The ocean escapes toward the sky. We smell its breath. We have taken the job we love of naming and I think it is a way of returning to paradise, this job of counting, of knowing who belongs to us. Everyone who is dear is named. It's how we keep alive, raising a quiet army against those who think they own the sky. I want you to know the best of us. The ones who can look you in the eye, and with the ocean as ally, I think even the man who prayed for the sun is eligible. We are few but we are also many and you can name us by our eyes.

In the beginning as we are walking on the beach, you run into a new friend to whom you said last night, "I'd like to see you again but it's not possible," and he answered, "Don't worry I'll find you." Now he's found you and we're on the beach together and you look each other in the eyes and we walk together by this sea which you say is like your ocean and by the sea where I an always walking when I am naming. It's dark now and the sun has fallen so far down behind the ocean that even if we stood on each other's shoulders on tiptoe on the pier we wouldn't be able to see it.

Still your son begins to draw on the dark sand. He draws a picture of Charlie Chaplin and we laugh at the turned out feet and the round eyes and he draws a big bubble which says *"Je suis Charlie Chaplin."* This is a few hours before we will hear that Chaplin has died but we don't know he's dead we're just walking along the beach meeting a friend who said he'd find you and your son's drawing a man with round eyes. This is the same beach that Charlie walked on and we remember Charlie and we laugh and you laugh because you can't forget anything and you recognize those round brown eyes because you never close your eyes to anything, not even the moment when I hurt you when you said, "We have already had so much if we didn't see each other again it would be enough." I said, "Yes, you're right but it still wouldn't be enough." And I hurt you. For you it has to be enough. It always has to be enough in the moment as it has to be enough for Charlie to have a pair of torn pants and a violin.

You're as homeless as he is and your country's under the fist of Charlie's bully and so you make a violin of poems and play on the street corners when you must.

But I'm greedy and also privileged to be able to want more and I want another day and consider asking the man who was praying to bring up the sun to give us another hour but I am still afraid of another miracle. I am thinking as I look at Charlie that I hope I will always have round open little brown eyes like Charlie's and I hope that I will always remember this moment, and I hope I will remember laughter that I will always . . . that it will be enough. . . . This is the moment they say that Charlie died and we don't know it and so we don't bury him. We are simply noting his presence with us as he catches our eye.

In the beginning we are walking on the beach and perhaps we are always walking on the beach until you will fly to Chicago. Chi-cago you say. Chi like the energy which the Chinese see and which we don't. We are walking on the beach and you are telling me about a woman who was healed by a bicycle. The bicycle of the revolution. You say the revolution is a shaman, that the revolution can heal even cancer. She's a student in your class and you healed her with a story about a bicycle as you healed my shoulder with just the slightest touch as you looked in my friend's eyes and knew he was a healer. He has it in his hands as you do, as we all must carry it in our eyes and hands because that way it's safe and no one can take it from us. No more than they can take the sea from us or the fact that we can see the sun at the same time from different continents and in that moment at eight in the morning and four in the afternoon we can see the sun as mirror and find each other in the reflection. They can't hold us apart though they think they can control our countries. You tell me the story of the healed woman who said, "You bicycled for my life like the cyclist in Antonio Skarmeta's story who bicycled for his mother's life, fighting death as he pumped his bicycle, his heart breaking up to the top of the mountain. His mother lived." You shared that story with the dying woman and told me Tonio had written it. I remember Tonio and how we looked into each other's eyes the last time we met. Everyone had given up the dying woman as everyone too often gives up on dying women, but you said "No, No, No. It's a lie. Death is a lie. Don't believe them. Believe you'll live." Pedaling. Pedaling. The heart pumping. You win.

We're walking on the beach while knowing that we don't quite have the revolution here to pedal for us yet. But we meet these friends on the beach who say they'll find us. And they do. That's a beginning. All the sets of eyes we found. You are pedaling for us and we are pedaling for you. When I was in Cuba there was a poster of Charlie Chaplin on a bicycle and he was pedaling, he was pedaling for *cinema movil*. They were taking the movies to the countryside to show them to peasants who had never seen movies in their lives and they were carrying the movies on big trucks that they set up in the fields at night under the stars and they took Charlie with them. He was pedaling for them. For the revolution.

You were flying to Chi-cago and we were in the airport elevator and an American man said "We're all going to the same place" and you were thinking "No we're not." And I had your bag on my shoulder and a black beret on my head and I was thinking that I looked like Tania the guerilla. She is dead. But my friend says I look like her and also says that I look like Ethel Rosenberg. When he feels loving, it is what he says. But Ethel is dead. And they say Charlie is dead. And we're not all going to the same place. And you said the year was full of death for you. It was the year that supposed friends turned against you. And the year was close to death for me. You said that you will never have a community again until you're home in Chile. But since I didn't die, I said, "My house is your house. *Mi casa es tu casa.*" You invited my friends in for dinner. Later, we came in from picking someone else up at the airport and you said, "We're home." And so we were. And if we never see the house again together it is enough because you're home in it. That can't end anymore than the sea can end or our eyes can end or the day we met in Santiago, Chile, and it was raining and the sun broke through suddenly and astonished our eyes.

I say, look at Charlie. He never said "never." And he was always playing the violin and crying as you were reading poems to me and crying and I went to the movies when you were gone and saw 1900 and cried and then I thought of Charlie who never said never, who never learned never. His gift to us. That he would be kicked out into the street. Beaten up. Robbed. Betrayed. Almost murdered and he always pedaled back, always jumped back up, bumped up like those foolish pop-up clowns that you can knock down but they pop-up, they can't be defeated if there's air in them. That is, if you've filled them with breath. Didn't you see Charlie pop-up on the beach? Did you think it was a gull? No. You took off your glasses and rubbed your eyes and looked at the sand with your glasses off seeing what your young son had outlined on the brown damp sand. *Je suis Charlie Chaplin. Soy Charlie Chaplin.* I am ... I am ... I am. ...

We're on the beach and it's barely raining but enough to know the drought is over and we're telling all the stories about all the ones we know. We are a few, so precious, so few I can count us on the fingers of my hand, but then I remember someone else and we are more and we name everyone we know in common, all the Chileans, and all the North Americans, and all the Latinos, and a few Europeans. We name all those we know in common because we're common people and we see eye to eye on this and we run out of fingers and go on to the next hand and run over all our fingers again counting as if we were tying knots in a string adding a knot for each one of us.

In the Huichol Indian ceremony a knot is tied into a string for each one who becomes part of the community. A knot for those who go forth and a knot for those who stay behind to tend the fire. I tie a knot in a string for you for the day when you go forth again and a knot in a string for me because I'll keep the fire. And when the peyote hunt is over they untie themselves from the strings. That is what the Huicholes do. Our Incan *quipo* strings are thick with knots as we talk. Inca counting systems. Storehouses full of grain. I believe it is a time of plenty. We have the seeds hidden and waiting. We count the names on our fingers one knot per name. We will plant the grain soon. In the meantime we keep the seeds between us. When you are a Huichol and you tie yourself into the string, you must confess everything. We tell each other everything we know.

Knotting. A sailor habit. We are by the sea. Soon we will sail back to Chile again. We are telling stories. The ocean comes up to us but it does not erase Charlie Chaplin. The breeze freshens as if to fill the sails which will carry us but the blowing sands do not cover Charlie Chaplin. We walk to the pier to look for the sun and find it gone and the merry-go-round is closed and you call your friends and they aren't home and then they are. The knots get thicker, heavier, fuller. There is more grain in the granary than we know. The *quipo* tell us it will last a long time. When the hunt is over we will not need to untie the knots. Those who tie in with us remain with us. When we met we became tied to each other. I didn't know why then. It was something about keeping our eyes open to each other. It was something about looking at each other in the eyes. It was something about Charlie Chaplin.

When we come home from walking on the beach there is a false news report. It says Charlie Chaplin is dead. Even *The Times* can lie. I hear it reported on the radio but the best sources can be in error. After all weren't we on the beach at the time of his alleged death, which means at that same moment we could have been looking at the sun together if it weren't raining. They say he died in Europe but how could that be? Didn't we see him smiling one foot angling toward the sunrise and one foot angling toward the sunset and an umbrella in his hand because of course it was raining. Before you came there had been a two-year drought and didn't we meet friends whom you thought you would never see again but one of them said quite casually the night before when you were in a room of fifty people and you looked us directly in the eyes to know if we were with you and we were, I think, almost all of us, and he said "I'll find you" and he did.

It had just started raining the night you came. Not a hard rain but enough to know the drought was over. Not hard like the very last night we met in Chile a year before the Coup and it was the *Dieciocho* and trouble beginning and when we stood in the downpour I said "*Nos vemos*" and you said "No. Not ever." And if you had said then "We have already had so much if we didn't see each other again it would be enough" you would have been right and wouldn't have been. It would not have been enough.

So don't flinch when I say it's not enough. I know it hurts you. I see it in your eyes. You look away wounded and lift your glasses, the shield you wear against seeing. There's nothing wrong with your vision. The glasses are like safety goggles. Don't flinch when I say it's not enough or when I give you Charlie when you say "never." It's only that I'm pedaling.

It was five years ago when we were standing in the rain, and we have met since and will meet again. Then you hadn't known you'd have to leave the houses you've had to leave. I can't count the houses you've been in since, how many in Paris alone and how many in Amsterdam and how many in how many countries since that day you said we'd never meet again. You've spent New Year's Eve in a different country every year and this year you say it's the first time you're in a house where someone has lived longer than a year and you say this was a year of death and pain a terrible year the worst since '73. You can't close your eyes to it. But you have lived almost a year in one house and have another year to go in it. You have two cats you hate but they live and require food; that is important. All of us need to remember that creatures live and require food and so we feed them. We all have death in our lives and we are scarred and we still live and we feed creatures, kids, and dogs and cats and friends and so we survive. We watch the ocean. You all have bicycles now in Amsterdam and can pedal like Antonio to the top of the mountain. Though your hearts may be broken, you pedal your bicycles to the mountain or to the market against death. We keep our eyes open all the time because we dare not shut them because then we would not be safe but with our eyes open we can see each other. That's the safety factor.

Do you remember we were walking on the beach in the beginning in a soft rain and I met a man who said he'd pray the sun up and you met a man who said he'd find you and then despite the news reports we saw a man with his feet pointing toward the horizons wearing a black hat and carrying an umbrella and the sea was full of fish and smelled like the *sopa de mariscos* we ate in Chile and the man said, "*Je suis Charlie Chaplin.*" We listened to him. Seeing him with our own eyes. Believing.

Secret and Hidden Intelligences

Secret and Hidden Intelligences:
Costa Rica Journal 1994

When the Teacher Comes

First you are confused,
then you make a mistake,
then you flee the scene,
or try to make amends,
then you remember
every day,

but only later do
you come to understand
that you were given a great gift
and nothing you might have done
could have prevented you
          from receiving it.

Costa Rica. A small hotel in Juntas at the foot of the washed out road to Santa Elena and Monteverde. The rain has been falling all afternoon on this green, lush and oppressive. Sitting in bed listening to the incessant drum of the water on the plastic roof, I argue with the climate. I say, though I was born by the ocean, later I became a desert woman. I say, I searched out my past and found a landscape for it. There is no water in my stars, I say. Earth and air have formed my mind, I insist. The sea has an edge but the water of the forest falls down upon you. Another kind of drowning. Still, I admit, this is true green. At home, the false green is dependent upon plastic bags of grass seed and the mechanical arms of sprinklers, is sold in rolls or squares, is laid down like linoleum on earth smoothed and polished like metal, all the rocks removed and packaged to be sold or dumped elsewhere. Then the grass rising up neat and trim as a military haircut, is kept in its place.

We stake out a table in a dark corner to escape the television in a Chinese restaurant near the main street. It may be over—not only civilization—but life. Each *comedor* boasts both television and music. There was a giant screen featuring music videos in the small bar across from the hotel in San Jose and we were assaulted by both rap music and *futball* in the *comedor* by *el mercado*.

Ten o'clock at night. Church bells amidst the shrill insect calls insistent as the warning of the rattler the Sunday before I left. "I am so scared," my granddaughter, Jamie, said. Her first clear sentence. As if she understood rattlesnake, as if she had no doubt about the dangers of the wild. They say fear of snakes, fear of falling and the dark are imprinted on the human brain. Not only humans, but animals too, experience fear. Each mammal senses its own life.

Dream

When I awaken, I go outside to walk on the cobbled streets of this village. The streets are flooded from the rains. A small brown river, all the water from the recent mountain storms runs past the hotel. I cross this river to the building opposite where a woman says that she has given up her life to do what she wants to do. "This conversation," I answer, "is a bridge between strangers."

There is no way back to the hotel without getting my feet wet. Great dark boulders shift under the swirl of the deep water. Memories of swimming in warm seas with my clothes on, rising with the cloth pressing against my skin and the small streams of water tracing the lines of my body.

Long peals of sound, monkeys probably, at the break of dawn. From the bathroom window, the first sighting of wildlife: Twenty vultures circling together in the sky. One turkey vulture soaring among them.

We make our way up the mountain, negotiating the rough clay and stony road. I am groping my way over to another side as well. There is a life back home I am trying to leave behind or heal. After all, this pervasive green is familiar, not alien.

I believe I've made a transition. Today adventure replaces yesterday's fear and confusion. The road has dried out and we negotiate the rough clay and stone, past the trucks, tractors, bulldozers repairing, repairing. The car lurches and rolls as we slowly ascend toward Monteverde, toward the preserve, toward the cloud forest. The honey, the passionate intimacy that we rely on between us returns. We have been apart for weeks and meet here in a different country in a foreign language. Now we try to shape our future, which Michael defines as the study of and return to the natural world.

This is the ritual of transition I have chosen to mark the end of my life as a psychotherapist. Even if I can't support myself as a writer, my life will never be the same. I will solve problems differently.

We have come to the crest. Lake Arenal shimmers in the distance amidst swaths of green. We both have a sense of new life. Ideas and passions interconnect like frenzied prokaryotes in joyous paroxysms over the exchange of genetic information. Marriage in the freedom of the first stages of evolution.

"I knew you weren't going home," Michael says. "You were just tired. Transitions some people never make in a lifetime, you made over twenty-four hours."

Now the land. Now the electric blue butterfly. Now birdsongs I have never heard or imagined. And now the rain. A steamy, relentless, thunderous deluge as we lay on the bed in our little *casita*, the door open as it pounds down. Rum and cokes. Chips of *plátanos*. Love making in the late afternoon before dinner.

What does one write about now? What still matters as life disintegrates into cyberspace? This longing not only for our mammalian selves, but for the animal itself as we devote our lives almost exclusively to the machine.

Andra Akers says a new tree has been developed that grows quickly and supplies food, paper, lumber, fuel. Every part of it can be used. It will be planted in rows like conveyors belts and assembly lines.

"What about the puma?" I ask.

I imagine a novel with lots of rain and a woman walking through a window into the trees.

I was afraid to come here. I was afraid to pass the placid green pastures that had once been forest. I was afraid to be with the dying earth, but Steven Kent said, "You don't leave a friend whom you can't heal. If your loved ones are dying, you don't abandon them. You stay very close the last months, weeks, days. You don't love them less if they are dying. In their last hour, you sit on the bed with them holding their hands."

Cloud forest Monteverde. The first day out we are caught in a rainstorm. Umbrella and poncho in the car, of course. It takes us three hours to return. It is exactly long enough to become both soaked and happy.

Strange calls. Birds or mammals, we can't tell. We hurry after them but see nothing. Occasionally songs of birds in the upper canopy. The wild life we do see: two centipedes, gold and black, one line of black ants and a patch of mosquitoes. I miss the mammals of the Sierras and color. Sometimes red berries, yellow flowers intermixed with the green.

I am energetic and agile despite the pain in my hips and legs. The branch twists out from the trunk, the vine torques, the matapalo winds tightly around a tree despite pain.

The bitch had breast cancer when I did. I am slow in the hip like the old timber wolf. I calculate the walking I intend and divide the years. How much time is left to walk through the disappearing forests on this earth?

We sink down in the wet soil, the mud holds us there. It is difficult to extricate ourselves. Red earth on our asses from all our slides and falls. Imagine what it would be to be planted here.

Ants marching in columns for miles, crowded one hundred feet abreast, hardly notice when one or another falls away.

Swift *arco iris*, rapid rainbow of two hummingbirds courting in flight, in dazzling whirrs and clicks, precise centrifugal whirls, figure eights, arpeggios as radiant as the inception of the universe, in an irresistible call and response of atoms, the love song of particles clustering. I marvel at the hum. The perpetual mmmmmm.

The beginning of life is recapitulated in the rain forest. Internal systems that resemble rainforest symbiosis. Ants and trees. Bat flowers. Microbe and plant. Microcosms and forest recapitulating each other.

A battle for light. Flora hide from the fierceness of the sun and then struggle toward it. Elaborate systems of defense and cooperation. Exchange of information, Lynn Margulis calls it. Forsyth and Miyata speak of the cycle of nutrients. The drama is visible: Obsession with borders. Development of protective sheaths and measures, barriers, toxins, deceits.

What has been eaten becomes venomous. Bitten leaves, embittered. Red signifies toxins. Tomatoes. The birds don't finish the fruit: The first taste, sweet; the last one poisonous.

Symbiotic exchange. Digesting each other's poisons. Exchange and inter-dependence. Allowing, even providing for, the existence of the "other."

The way the other, mitochondria, for example, are incorporated into the self. Allurements in a vast and complex interchange, the passion of growth and decay. Dung beetles forage in shit, returning it to the chemical soup.

Prigogine says each century develops its own science shaped by the receptivity and prohibitions of culture. Are we willing to relinquish the monistic view? How do we allow everything its own life without colonizing it, abdicate the belief that the human is the one dominant chosen species to gain a perspective of dynamic interchange? The end of monotheism, monoliths, monopolies, monarchy and monotony.

The teaching of the rainforest. Diversity and randomness. Species do not cling together. Seeds are scattered far and wide. Conditions for growth do not exist next to the parent that having reached the light creates shade for those beneath; the seed must sow itself elsewhere.

The light gap. A tree falls and everything in the area falls over it. Then each organism reaches up, seizes the unexpected chance for sunlight and streaks up to the sky. Michael was talking about the fall of the Soviet Union, then I saw it: the fallen tree, the light gap and the internecine struggles.

A bird alights on a branch. Dip and flurry of leaves. It could be the wind. It can always be wind rushing past, something invisible chasing after the invisible, then or before, a red beak or a flash of blue, yellow green, black, orange. Elaboration of the improbable. Color tunnels through the air, streaks of tinted light not unlike trills and chords.

El Jardin de las Mariposas. The garden of the butterflies. Gold and jade cocoons. Madagascar moon moths. Eurema Dina. Owl butterflies. Giant cobalt blue Morpho butterflies. *Babochka* [Russian]. *Chocho* [Japanese] *Parpar* [Hebrew]. Butterflies everywhere in the small hothouses and net tents.

Only a streak of an animal. Fur. Gray or brown. Leaves crunched, then no sound. The presence of the animal in the absolute silence it creates about itself. From its hidden place, the animal watches us. It has one question: "Are these two human beings dangerous to me?"

And there they are. The mythic birds. The endangered, resplendent Quetzals.

I want to catch all with a name. Fix this bird to the branch with a nail: Emerald toucanet, slaty tailed toucan, long tailed manakin, yellow throated euphonia, blue-crowned motmot, turquoise cotinga, the resplendent quetzal. A painter could see the bird without the name, but for the writer, it is only half seen.

This is the place between lives. At home, I will move down into the word, settle into the task of the single sentence.

El Bosque de los Ninos Monteverde. The Children's Rainforest. It costs $45 to buy an acre of land to add to the rain forest. If in the course of a lifetime, each individual in the world financed the return of one acre. . . ?

At sunset, a young woman walks up the rocky street, torches of ginger flowers in her hand. This exquisite edge between satisfaction and longing.

The owner of the restaurant has propped a envelope decorated with balloons and toy bears against a glass jar of red roses and the words "*A mi amor.*"

"*Seis meses,*" he says, "*Seis meses, nueve dias, y quatro horas. Mi amor.*"

The edge between the wild and the domestic. The shabby place where breakdown does not dissolve into the sweet humus of decay. I sit on the toilet in the dark so I won't see the stains on the tile that was once bright terra-cotta splattered with brilliant white and yellow, colors of butterscotch and caramel, now covered with a tedious patina of dust. So I won't see the irregular caves and crevices where the plaster is worn and eroded, or that the wood on the ceiling is smeared with careless brush strokes of white wash. Or that the seams don't meet and in the cracks ants, wasps, moths, beetles, roaches have colonized the terrain. The beetle sniffing its way across these asphalt tiles is not the same beetle on its rightful path on the forest floor. When we turned over the moving leaf and found indigo dung beetles in the amber pool of excrement, we were not offended. But if someone had shit here on the floor. . . .

How different if this were a hut of bamboo with a roof of fern leaves? A platform hidden in the middle canopy? A round cave in the lattice of the fig tree? Imagine an architecture based upon animal housing. Underwater apartments in the mode of beavers. Long narrow bedrooms carved out of tree trunks and bark. Great stone rooms. Cities enclosed in translucent globes like the dwellings of wasps or burrowed in the ground under conical domes like termite ants. So much contrived since we came down out of the trees.

Dream
A miniature. I am shown earth packed against a tiny stone wall. Those below have sown plants that will sustain me for the rest of my life.

Each day we walk in a different part of the rain forest. Here we are led by the three notes of the toledo. *To Le Do.* Then toucans, agoutis, coatimundis. And the strange gray-necked wood rail. Gray neck, brown nape, olive mantle, cinnamon breast, black belly, chartreuse bill, red iris, coral legs.

I had expected the rain forest to be fierce. I had expected danger and adversity. At the outset I had wanted to turn back, had feared the road, had imagined obstacles and the enmity of strangers. But here the mist descends as a blessing, the butterflies are transparent, the hidden birds are ceaseless in their music and the reassuring and pervasive green is interrupted by flashes of red, black, yellow, indigo, cerulean, gold, copper and lapis. I know how to write grief but I do not know how to render this beauty that gentles those who live among it.

One subatomic particle transforms into another. An essential dance as energy is exchanged and released. Repeated everywhere. The development of microcosms. Procaryotes and then eukaryotes break down essential compounds to release the six essential elements that combine and recombine in creation: hydrogen, nitrogen, carbon, oxygen, sulphur, phosphorus. Growth and decay. Not life and death but order and organization, deconstruction, disorder and reorganization. Form, disorder, form. Constant combination and recombination. Constant change. Form and emptiness. The enigma of discovering self in the constantly shifting patterns, unity in the metamorphosis.

The brown butterfly disguised as a dead leaf has found the banana I set in the crook of the tree and has buried itself in it. Sunlight releases the honey in the fruit. Here is a little world: Butterfly, fruit, sun. Variations on yellow and brown. The trunk and the bark of the tree, also dark amber in color. The warm silence in the fall of the direct light here at the center of the earth. Yes, here is the world. The clouds have parted. Butterflies, color of chestnut, mahogany, maple, walnut, oak. The light, the golden light that brings it all to life. Shadow and glow out of the living cocoon, unfurling from ingots of copper and gold. At the base of the tree, the dark, wet leaves curling up, soft folds tightening again into the earth even as the butterflies open their drying wings. Flashes of gold everywhere. Oranges, yellows and ivory in flight. Fireflies by night and the rust of the damp stump and the ripening fruit in the saffron light. I am drinking black tea with cream, color of tusk and bone. My skin is tanned leather and so the honey runs.

Stella's bakery. Breakfast in the garden. Morning glories and princess flowers.

The only people I meet on the path of *Baja del Tigre* are surprised by a woman hiking alone. What is there to fear in the rain forest? Are they still afraid of the territorially deprived, hunted-almost-to-extinction wild cat?

Fernando Valverde of the Santa Elena Reserve says *El Bosque*, the forest wants to return. Plants, he says, know if you care about them. Animals scrutinize us only to learn one thing— whether we will do them harm. Is the human being a friend or an enemy?

At this moment when I cannot tell the difference between the world and what I love; the world rests in benevolence. The leaf, which was still, bends in response to my gaze as if the wind had come. Or the leaf moved first and my eye caught the movement and it came to life as if the light had come. Who dares presume she knows the direction of love? Who dares assume will? Why not imagine the love of the leaf? I am finally wide-eyed enough to see it. Pami Blue Hawk said, if you gaze at a leaf lovingly, the leaf will move as if the wind is carrying it. But something else. The leaf has been gazing at me. It has been waiting, most patiently, for me to open my eyes. It has hoped that I would see.

When we were still enough, when we had sat without moving for several hours, the birds did come, exactly when the veil of mist descended. It isn't that the veil parts here. The veil descends and one can see, finally, one thing at a time. There's the swallow-tailed kite in its smooth orbit and here is the one note of the three-wattled bellbird. A small patch of yellow flowers, butterflies, white, blue, golden or brown, floating alone. A small shrub with a few red berries hidden in the trees. In the profusion of green, every creature unmistakable in the pursuit of its own life.

Two black guans roosting in the top canopy, feeding on strings of pale yellow berries.

We do not gather berries here. We do not net the butterflies. We do not pick the flowers or search for bones or shards. We bring home no teeth, no trophies. Not even a branch or a leaf. We learn to take nothing into our own hands. This thumb has brought us to grief. I want to relinquish the history of these hands.

An extraordinary song emerges from the twilight mist. Trills, whistles, cascades, warbles. It could be the nightingale. The ruddy-capped nightingale thrush. Mozart, a small brown inconspicuous bird, the magic flute in the underbrush.

The daily food. *Casada*, Marriage plate: beans, rice, *plátanos*, salad. This daily simplicity is the marriage feast.

Dream.
Jonathan Omer-man has acquired a magical device that will disappear us from this urban scene in the glint of a firefly. As soon as our essential business is completed, we will vanish.

Perhaps we will not leave Monteverde. Perhaps we will never leave Costa Rica. I could sit on this porch a long time learning the birdsongs. The one haunting note, metal clanging against metal, as of a buoy at night, or a goat bell in the Greek hills. Then the chatter of squirrels leaping from tree to tree. I want to die here.

Dream.
Though I'm feeling under the weather, I will take care of Jamie, my three-year-old granddaughter. When she comes in, I say, "I'm feeling vulnerable."
"Where?" she asks.
"In my heart," I answer.
"That's good place," she affirms.

The animals: it is not their intelligence that has been lacking, but ours; we—adults, humans— withhold our intelligence from the exchange.

We begin to feel part of this little Spanish and Quaker community. Michael was reading to me from A. S. Byatt's "Conjugal Love" as we sat on the couch of the little inn across from the bookstore and coffee shop where our laundry was drying. The owner of the Daikiri Restaurant selected a few exotic jungle flowers from the bookstore vases and carried them, like banners, back to his restaurant.

The owner of the bookstore is despondent as is the man who lets us walk his trail, *Sendero Escondido*. The European-American melancholy is endemic while the *Ticos* somehow seem happy with their lives. When the young man got off his motorcycle at the bottom of the stairs, he smiled generously as if it were a pleasure to say hello.

Michael defines the village as the ecotone between civilization and the wild where everyone is afraid of being eaten. Unlike other species, we are not locked into the dance of predation with one or only a few other species. We are the predators of all species. We fear everything, consume everything. We take all the habitats. We separate body, house, village, city from the wild.

Freedom, we call it, but nothing is free of our presence. Even here in the cloud forest, the per-petual whine of cars, trucks, AVCs, motor bikes. A car brought us here. We drive to the entrance of the forest each day. There is no relief here from our penetrating mechanical sounds.

We are driving in our car when we come upon the sloth. Another car stops as well, and only when the woman grumbles, "*Feo, feo*," does her companion turn off the headlights that are skewing this sloth to the center of a public drama. But still the four of us are riveted by the creature struggling toward safety under our gaze. Soon, I am ashamed of my curiosity, of my intrusion into the life of an animal, whom I do not begin to understand, and with whom I am incapable of interacting reciprocally. Michael and I quickly re-enter the car and make a hasty exit, turning our lights on only when we are a good distance away.

The wet and mud bedraggled sloth
clambering its slow and deliberate way
up the slippery embankment
claw over claw
limb over limb

despite the glare of headlights
and the unremitting stare
of humans
transfixed before
the biological agony
of helplessness and
tedious survival,

still climbs
doggedly,
determinedly,
perhaps stupidly
toward the illusive leaves,
and an essential branch,
some height
there, up there
in the rain
there in the wet,
moon obscured
night.

As all I can do
is protect this creature
from my own kind.

Dream
There is a task to be accomplished. It has to do with the ship. I don't know how to get it
to a mooring in the center of a large waterway. It is seemingly a living thing. Even now as
I record the dream I feel affection for it. Unable to get to the first mooring, I lead it down
a narrow channel but there is no place for it here. We must turn around. A new difficulty
presents itself. If I leave it here, I have no way of returning. I am incapable of swimming
across the sea. Moreover, it is night and cold. I can see that I will probably drown.

On the way to *Sendero Escondido*. A shrine of tires half buried in a garden. Stonehenge in
black rubber.

The future is not before us.
First it hid,
then it doubled back.
It's there

behind us,
and not waiting for us.
Don't be mistaken,
it's running away.
It wants to be free of us.
It also wants to live.

Thunder in the distance. The mist coming in quickly, damp and still. Rain and everything will run in mud.

The resonant call of the howler monkeys and an answer from far away in the woods. The great male awakens us. Dawn reveals him in the crook of the tree and in a lower branch a clutch of adults lean against each other, occasionally stroking each other while the young climb up and down excited by day.

The Small Brown Gods

Because we called them silently. Because we were longing for them the way we are beginning to long for our ancestors, for these small lithe brown gods who live among the leaves. Because we walked down to the edge of the green gorge where the fresh water filtered through the branches of fern trees before spilling onto the ground becoming river, the monkeys came. First only the limbs of the trees bending under their weight, but enough of a sign.

When we remained still, they sent one the long distance across the canyon to walk swiftly over our heads. The elder female disappeared as if she had not seen us, but then I heard a silent summons to the great fig tree in the interior that stretched through the four canopies toward the sky.

We were not to climb it. We were not to claim it. We were not to eat its fruit. We did not know if it would nourish or poison us, if it is the tree of death or the tree of life. We sat by the great roots, as instructed, and wondered if we would ever be permitted to return to knowledge.

And then they came in procession. The female leading the others toward us. The trees bowing under them as they clambered above us, one after another, most solemnly. The small brown gods with the white faces of saints.

Time vanishes. There are various names for the disappearance: History and Loss or Eternity and Paradise. In History, we are separate, but in Paradise we are together.

Then a young, blond girl came strolling down the path, flicking her ponytail, proud and oblivious, chattering loudly to her companions of adventures and accomplishments, naming the animals.

In that instant, fifty million years re-arranged themselves again like great stones on the tedious road of exile.

The small brown gods withdrew. Dogs barked querulously at the perimeter of the reserve. Above us the invisible bellbird honked monotonously in the tree and the thick, dull fog descended as everything vanished from view.

We spend the day at the end of *Bajo del Tigre*. All day we are there alone. A rambunctious squirrel skittering down a branch is startled by my presence. Stops. Freeze frame. Eyes bulging. Fear? Curiosity? Fear, I decide. I begin to hate myself, my species.

It is rapidly becoming dark when we hike out. For a short while we can barely see where we are going on the narrow dirt path and just when we are becoming a little uneasy because the canopy is so thick and multilayered that only a small portion of the sunlight ever reaches the floor, we come out into a clearing where once again we glimpse the last of the rosy golden light. Silhouetted in a tree are four black guans, unusually silent, their tail feathers long and sleek against the branches of the tree, curved heads and crooked necks turned elegantly toward the setting sun. In the painted dreams of Chinese emperors, in illuminated manuscripts, on painted Byzantine ivories, I have seen the reverie of such birds, carefully drawn to imply their song. But what communion do these birds share as they—as we—pause at the end of the day to watch the descent of light?

Now it is so dark, we cannot see the path. I am not afraid. Every now and then fireflies ignite and we go forward.

Night. A *cerro* of rubble—cement, concrete, stones—in the corridor between the Pizzeria for the locals and the equally poor *tienda*. A little mountain of human offal that will never decay that the small and excited mongrel puppy climbs to declare his delighted sovereignty. A young man speeds up from the road on his motorcycle, wings his leg across the seat and stands there. Man and dog confront each other. The dog is insistent. The man finally smiles and the dog yields his mountain.

The *tienda*. A rectangle of light. An open door. Four people seated in a line on wood kitchen chairs, looking upward, smiling. From the vantage point of my car window, I see the other square of light, higher on the dark green wall, smaller, to the right of the yellow cast of the open doorway. There beyond the grid of iron bars to prevent burglars from entering and stealing who knows what—green glass bottles of *Concha y Torro* from Chile, locally manufactured *plátanos fritos* packed in flimsy plastic bags without labels, laundry soap, a case of *cerveza, Imperial Costaricense*—is another green rectangle of light. The television. A commercial for Honda. A tropical island. A blond white woman, perfectly suntanned, in a dress that never wrinkles, springs like Venus from the sea, arms outstretched, cleavage, V for Victory. She leaps out of the immaculate car to explore the wonders of the immaculate jungle, the immaculate sea, the immaculate palm-studded beach of an immaculate tropical country. Let's call it Costa Rica.

Michael emerges with two bottles of wine that the storekeeper opened and re-corked. As he opens the car door and the dim light flickers, I can't help but see that the skin on my hand between the thumb and the second finger is folding softly, like my father's hands as he aged. I am wearing silk pants and a silk blouse which, I noticed when I dressed this evening even by the light of a single bulb, have several tiny holes from wear. Garments softly wrinkled like my hands. We put the bottles on the car floor and Michael backs the car, Hyundai, silver gray, streaked with dust, rain water, mud, up toward the pile of crushed stone, old pavement, abandoned building materials and we take off toward *el Restaurante El Bosque* where we will eat *ensalada de palma* without caring or noticing in the dim light the wood warping away from the tiles, the gap between the wooden door and the door jamb, the cracks around the sink and the cutting boards where the food is prepared outside of our view.

Just after the caterwauling on our doorstep when I told Michael I cannot bear another conversation about apocalypse, a plume of fire and noxious gas shoots up into the air. The apparently ersatz metal vase, 65 *colones*, 42 cents, that we were using as a candleholder has caught fire. But when I open the door to put it outside, we see, for the second time tonight in our crises of descent, the full moon and her attendant clouds awhirl about her, and gradually increasing and diminishing swirling coronas of golden and silver light.

It is midnight. I put on my shoes and throw a pale blue-gray silk scarf from the Island of Lesbos over my shoulders pretending my white nightdress is a summer frock. We dance and fall over on the carefully mowed lawn, then stumble down the stony road connected to each other by the earplugs of a walkman. Stéphane Grappelli and George Shearing. Violin and blind piano. *Makin' Whoopee*. Michael is barefoot, his pants rolled up and our shadows in the moonlight . . . who knows? Charlie Chaplin and his beloved at the end of Modern Times, the ruffles of her white nightgown billowing against her thighs, his cuffs, jaunty. Climbing over a low concrete wall, cautious of the stakes of rebar, we lie down on the mist damp grass and watch the clouds boil lovingly around the full moon, then dissolve into the midnight sky of the valley. Dissolve into each other, dissolve and emerge.

I almost relax into his arms. I am almost ready to undress myself from the despair of human shabbiness and pollution. Almost ready to yield to the raspy and poignant violin, and the slight askew and plaintive variations on the piano. A duet of cloud and moon, vapor and stone, moving, unmoving. I put my head on the shoulder of the man who is lying quietly ecstatic on this side of a threshold where decay remains the pungent dark movement of earth back into form.

Again and again, the salvation of the endlessly moving clouds and the appearance of the slow-moving, freewheeling swallow-tailed kites. Again and again, the ceaseless black and white birds gliding above us circling in the same motions as the continuous transformation of sky. And the silence comes down again without anger from the blessed canopy of night. I, myself, rising finally, like the gray wisps of fog in its endless movement upward.

As if it is the beginning of the world, the radiant clouds come swirling toward us in a ferment of light and ever changing mist. His infinite and artful metamorphoses. Light, tinted by reflection: gold, red, pink, flamingo, salmon, then gull gray and night. The paternal dance of wispy ecstasy upon the slow changing body of the mother in her subtle and infinite variations of green, brown and green again. The grace and delicacy of the mist—impish, insubstantial, fragile—stepping, oh so nimbly, upon cataracts of leaves and water, dark heaving sands, the fluid, substantial, ample, oh so abundant passion of the body earth.

Shadow Letters:
Self Portrait of a Woman Alone

This persistent search for the answer is perhaps itself a
constant flight from wonder.

—Albert Einstein

Valyermo: Naomi

Women alone get the pickings from others' lives. Yet gleaners served a function. Look how faithful Ruth was to Naomi.

These months we have been out of phase. Two of the fourteen moons of Jupiter, we do not turn at the same speed though we keep our orbit. You say you carry me in your heart over any distance. But what crosses these dead seas?

Since I have had to go out of the gates of the city to fight for love, I have named myself "Warrior." I am not tired, but I have lost the ability to win. This day is called retreat. On my walk, broken foundations of deserted houses built only with what the mountains offer. In this desert, let me find a house of my own with a fireplace of stone. If I must be alone, let it be with the elements.

When we first met, you had been drumming in the dry hills. Yesterday, I drummed alone at the crest. The student of the Kalahari said, "The desert healers are men though some women have made that journey into the other world." But men can't heal unless the women sing.

Men drum and women sing. Women singing for each other as well.

In the Kalahari, the older women build a nuptial house of sticks and then the couple lies down. If I could do that for you, now that you are coupled, it is because your singing has eased me. That is how I know what sacred is.

When I asked, the I Ching answered, "Gathering Together." I can find nothing but lupine and dry twigs. Living alone, I must provide my meat and my protection. Territory says, I should become a huntress. You say, we are past the age of Artemis, and custom says, it is women who gather and the men who hunt. I go across the desert with empty hands. The hawks circle overhead. Nothing remains.

Cape Cod: Caitlin

Two days wondering what I will write to you. Hoping to read something in these letters of tea leaves and divining by the footprints of birds. The crystal turns slowly in the alphabet of light. The windows steam over, then bead. The drops of water running down are postcards from the universe. I can't read the messages. I have no patience, never learned to knit, to twist long hours into wool, even to keep warm. I do not know how hemp holds ships in line.

Today I walk to the dunes. Tomorrow, I return to find my own tracks and follow them again. A friend says, "Your journey is going home again." At dawn the dunes say, "No one has been here before." Everything disappeared as a man might into your hair.

I am wandering down to water. I was born by the sea, but my father was not a sailor. I do not know how to live out what comes to me in storms. These days I learn north and bitter and fjord.

I take the earth in my mouth. Welcome mad girl who eats soil. I saw the wind's nest on the promontory. There is more light here in the gray sky than broken into colors, and the trees spread themselves secretly across the darkness. I think you know these distances of sea, moor and plain. It is not night, but the gray implacable dawn calling me to truce as the tide always calls the sun.

I think you're blond through dealing with this harsh light. All fishermen are the colors of salt. Dark mariners drown. The men I've loved have been the color of rope.

Gather me into your stout nets.

Cambridge: Joyce

In the dream, it is I who give birth. You know how birth is. It insists.

The body has its own necessity; it does not ask permission of the mind. In my house, the wolf bitch digs a den in the darkest corner and howls to her non-existent pup.

Soon, the vet says, she will bring milk to her emptiness. Birth does not require progeny. We have a right to nurture nothingness.

Afterwards, in my dream, I am the one who gives birth. But when we meet, it is your daughter I see born on film. What comes out of us is for all our eyes. You could show birth to me once more and then again. The entire night passed with her emergence. You say the film was a call to what you had lost.

In the dream, afterwards, it is I who give birth. The birth is always the same. The child is invisible and must be taken by the hand. This is about hands.

In the cold streets, you put your hand in the pocket of my coat when we meet after twenty years. The door of your house opens to me as if it were never locked. I have returned to my beginnings in order to set out again. What I took with me from my childhood was forgetfulness. What you had in your palm was pain. As children, we stood outside the circle with each other.

To come home, I must learn where I first saw my own footsteps. At fourteen, I had a double loneliness of the body. You didn't know about my wandering at night. We shared the daytime, but after midnight, I roamed the beach learning the dialect of the sea. Later, I gave my body to lovers, hoping to drown. Here the ocean is wild, aggressive and merciless. My hair is silver. We have never known each other as women before.

I live in the shade of trees broad at the base like women who open themselves to oxen and buffalo. Where you live, the trees are slim as your daughter. The birch is shy and about to be given in marriage. The eucalyptus says, "Your silver hair is older than mine." My body is an old whore and the moon pulls me. In the restaurant, my friend says, "You can't go home." The old dog will die of the whelp's need.

Twenty years ago, you thought I had betrayed you when I had a child. Now you are ready. The old dog is dying. Yesterday, we cut out her breast. In her last moments, she and I are more than sisters. I say, I don't believe in symmetry or trying to create beauty out of pain. The young wolf will not be alone. Her blood tells her, "Run in packs." I also howl the night in the cold bed.

What can we count on after twenty years? The ocean. And our ability to walk alone. I am reduced to this belief.

Provincetown: Barbara

This is called Land's End. The slow tide covers the prints of little feet. Prepare for the underwater sleep. Temporarily, I am living in the house of illuminated fish, stumbling alone, arms extended through the phosphorescent dark.

In the night, the dream passes for the embrace of two hands. In the day, I hold a walking stick. You live in another country where I used to know the weather.

Under the sea, the typhoon plays a harp of kelp. The song is lament. Rain cannot reach me at a thousand fathoms. I am afraid I will forget to brush my hair. What vial and which waters will I find to carry this message to you?

Be alert for sailors and the drone of buoys and the man who dove into the sea for us and brought up our key. There must be a door here even in these depths.

This morning, my father said, "I am the loneliest man in America." But Bim had nowhere in the universe to receive mail. A long time ago, he taught us shipwreck. In this drowning, can I remember my name?

Provincetown: Jane

My hands in your coat. The skins are small and no one identifies the smooth and tiny animal. Something I cannot name keeps me warm. I am practicing loneliness, become a virtuoso. In my old age, I will be prepared for what I can not bear but will wear like this old coat, the one you gave me that warm season, in preparation for winter. Where we live, the snows do not blow between our fingers.

There is no laughter in the single country, and I am given cramped rooms. One had no light and two beds, and here the room lined with books is smaller than my pen. Outside this room, among the ferns and orchids, couples sit in wicker chairs in the afternoon sun of idle conversation against which I open and close the doors. The room is improvised for a maiden aunt or other odd creatures. Herons and cranes could nest here. I have seen the pain braiding through your straw hair.

This may be the last of my inexplicable solo voyages. This morning, I thought of all the times we walked the beach. You would like it here. The dunes loom like great white breasts on the hides of elephants. Nipples of thunderous beasts. Why don't we live in herds?

You never travel alone. Wisdom doesn't protect me, doesn't remind me that dreams are only night friends. We could breakfast together in this inn as the stained glass calls in the light—burgundy, gold, cobalt blue. The gulls say wind is to be passed through. I cannot pass through my own heart.

Thoreau wrote a book about the Cape and I came here hoping this solitary would find her own shadow on the sand pleasing. Thoreau lived alone and sang about it, but in my wandering, I have found pleasure only where there is absolutely no one at all, not even myself.

These letters are about loneliness and persistent attempts to eat alone with grace. The meal is possible if I imagine I am beautiful. About handsome women—one assumes they have choice.

A friend said, "Everyone in the world is coupled. The universe is Noah's ark and those without a mate will drown." At night in restaurants, I think of suicide, but in the morning, the poem holds out its hand.

As you would guess, the inn is haunted. They say the ghost of a woman wanders in the rooms. She hung herself from the rafter, just below the Chinese goddess of evil who breathes in the dark. Yet the mornings are ferns, blue glass and orchids. Gulls catch the afternoon light.

Tomorrow when no one speaks, I can have a love affair with gulls. Where are you wandering? Your daughter loved horses and lives at home. A man has never rubbed her body down. We were broken into early. Perhaps I am an empty bowl, one of the old shards so valuable to museums. I do not like afternoon tea though visits are the life I have. Promise not to let me do this again.

On the dunes, I wonder when you will leave home. The snow is falling but does not stick to the ground. Salt from the sea erodes what comes down. When I was a kid, rock salt on the sidewalks against the ice.

A man built this inn as an aerie and afterwards never ventured out. Though I've tried to build a house of life with my hands, I'm left to be the chronicler of carpenters. Are you leaving just as I call myself Spinster, and settle into the smallest possible room?

The Demon Country

Invocation

Some of us have spent our lifetimes
searching our bodies
for the letters of flame,
when they arise,
some of us burn
and some of us set fires.

Canta

In the dream you dream, you hear what the Taoists dream,
the Kabbalists, the shamans, that sound, lost in the universe,
the broken syllables, cacophony calling the great seekers,
to find the signature in bark, in babble,
in the scratch of reeds, slough of water down the slimy rock,
holding the great lost song in its shimmering descent,
the shattered sentences of the dumb gods
brooding in the babble, in baboon chatter, in the buzz,
an egg, blue, size of my thumb, broken open, jagged,
a dappled hide, a pictograph of ferns
might be that vowel, echo of the desperate incantation,
                    Beresith
Need, need, need for a new invocation:
                    Let there be light!
against the darkening of blood, the chaos
of the crosshatch of wounds, the turmoil
of broken spines and broken speech,
the apostasies of mutant torturers,
the amputations of body and soul,
the . . .

I'm certain it is only one word, one sound, one breath,
we had it once, Claribel, it was ours,
we lost it, forgot it, it was broken from us.
It is very dark without that word.
Sometimes the poem provides a little light, a matchstick
sufficient to continue the search,
but the scratch of the match releases sulfuric recognitions,
the smell of land burning, human hair crackling in flames,
indifferent tortures, slavery.

Somewhere in that other country without territory or passports,
the dead are waiting behind the barbed wire of air,
trying to signal the one word into us,
they were also deaf when they were here—
they could not recognize the word in the shape of hands,
in the mute arrangement of molecules in the marrow,
in . . .

The gods say,
we have only to speak it once only to read it, only to see it,
only . . .

It's a small thing, but we don't, we can't; the wars continue.
Everything is death without that word.

The gods turn aside, having sung once to us,
then out of pity scatter shards of song among the seed pods
for the harvest of one note.

After the word, we will breathe together,
another kind of eloquence,
death only in its own time,
all of us expiring like leaves
falling in such ruddy gentleness.

Till then, the necessity to speak, also in sleep,
to speak as if each word might be that cry,
to hold nothing back,
to search the language of every living thing,
also the chant of stones,
a cry every thousand years,
—now a promise—
even my heart opening as if it were a mouth.

Confirmations

One
There are, after all, children.

Two
Let us begin at the beginning.
The elements are
air earth fire water.
Do you need more
considering
that there are children?

Three
Initially
a wind to a twig,
brushfire,
rain yesterday,
burial plot today.
The elements play many games.

Four
Within the branches
birds nests of dry twigs.
Against the bellows
half a dozen eggs a day.
Yellow beaks against the rain.
Look in the bulrushes
for the children.

Five
The women have such longing
as if
there were not enough children
to nestle against them.

Six
Sometimes,
after a war
there are
still
children.

Which of These Forms Have You Taken?[16]

This year I have been growing
down into the tree
against my will
making nothing happen.
Across the woods
through the bare branch haze
of bars against the light
someone is coming with an axe.

I have known this all my life.

16   Title from "A Soul, Geologically," by Margaret Atwood, in *Selected Poems*.

Wolf Leave Tracks Now[17]

The animal looking out of the bars
is relieved to know she is an animal
but nevertheless they have put her
behind bars,
when they look at her through bars,
they become the bars, so to speak,
look how they spread themselves out
between the dark poles,
she does not want to be those bars
but she is behind them nevertheless,
she is pleased she is an animal,
but she also knows
she is behind bars,
she,
who would not know
how to construct bars,
she is an animal,
that is what she knows,
she is the animal,
that is
what she knows,

she knows
the animal,
she knows.

---

17   Title of poem from "Climbing the Ridge," by Judith Minty.

Griefmaking

Light,
just the moment before falling,
blazes in the rye grass
and sets a fire in the eye.
Flood of afternoon light
in the moment before dying,
before the coming of the dark,
purple of the open blossom
against the green,
lattice of leaves
against the sky
in the darkening of the coming storm,
evening falling so soon after dawn.

The redwoods once had enough time
to know what they have to know,
now feel the terrible press
of relentless time bearing down.

Wanting to get my bearings
on this sorrow,
wanting what cannot be given,
    —a caesura—
to prepare for what is coming,
to prepare to make the offering of self
to whatever is asking for us.
Wanting to hold on to something
in the advent of loss.

It is all our own doing,
this storm of our own making.
Here comes the tempest,
when we are not prepared for rain.

Endarkening

If darkness
—black ice of the universe—
punctured the day sky,
—coal needles piercing
the blue numinous air—
if the Northern Darks
were the sacred fingers of noon
and a black rain fell
—dusty and iridescent—
on my lover's black hair,
on all the crows and ravens . . .

Could we love the light less?
Could we learn to explode the darkness?
Then the death of slow ashes
would cover us quietly,
and this terrible white fire
would not last forever
in our banked radiant bones.

Iron Horses

Peter Matthiessen says,
"In the wilderness,
the human voice
is disturbing to animals
we might otherwise see."

The whinny of the iron horse,
echoing over the mountains,
warning of its approach,
announcing its departure,
is drowning out
the snort of some great beast,
a moose, probably,
who has hidden himself
in thickets that have arisen
out of burned earth,
storm and lightning,
forty years ago.

Species, we designate as weeds,
invade and colonize a space,
allowing no others
but themselves.
The iron horse is one of these,
imperious in his vast territory,
without enemies,
wary of being mounted,
fearless and dominant.

Unsubjugated
by the iron horse,
only the maniacal bleat
of the tiny towhee
coming alone
to the scattered seed and grain.

Soundscape in these remote
mountains, this wilderness:
tires on gravel, a cow or goat bell
as in the most civilized Greek hills.
Conversations from afar: "I can't hear you."
"Never mind."

Dogs barking incessantly,
day and night,
the iron horses galloping,
forty a day,
and tourists gawking.

I have chosen
of all possible gifts,
a bardo of silence
so that I can learn
what I have not learned
in seventy years. But,
try as I may
I cannot find my way to stillness.

"The summers are short here,"
the woman says. The summers,
this time, my life,
how short they all are.
And shorter still
as the trains carry
everything away,
on their metal wheels.
In their boxcars,
endless transport
of different matters,
of what was once alive,
to places and uses unknown.

On my last day,
after hiking in the mountains
in the early morning,
when I had hoped, for once,
to escape the horse,
I heard the metal yodel
of his horn echoing.
Then a wild cantata
of Coyote song reverberated
from the summit,
as if to still him
once and for all.

Crimes Against Soft Birds[18]

Today I met a woman who was tortured in Chile.
Tomorrow I will write a letter about another woman
who is being tortured now.
When I write this I am thinking
I want the pain to stop,
but I don't know whose pain can be interrupted or how.

How can I write about her pain?
I can only imagine what it must be to be torn apart
and to heal with the anger within,
to be left with a bit of knife inside.

This is a poem for women I do not know
whose cells are barred by dogs with electric teeth,
men with blades for arms,
grotesques from other wars,
who are entrenched here, digging in.

The women I know are so soft,
they have breasts to cry against,
when they put out their arms, they are beaches,
sand, mouths like silver fish,
voices of kelp crisp and clear.

Where do we go
where do we go to a sea that is safe
for the soft sand that sifts and blows?

She said,
I was an American; I was treated well.
They drove me through the city with my breasts exposed,
they kept me blindfolded thirteen days without bread and water,
solitary, except when they entered to threaten rape.
I was alone in the dark, except
when they tortured someone next to me.
I was alone in the silence

---

18   Amy Conger, an American art historian, was arrested in Chile October, 1973, tortured, threatened with
death, forced to ride naked through the streets, catapulted downstairs while blindfolded, deprived of water, denied
sleep and forced to stand until she was exhausted. At the time of writing this poem, April 1975, she was devoting
her time to making the facts known about torture in Chile, the absence of human rights, and U.S. involvement in
the coup.

except for the animal howls next to me.
I was alone in my cell
when they attacked.

She said,
After they raped the women, stuffed them with dogs and rats
broke their vaginas with electric shock,
they kissed them, petted them tenderly,
as if a woman was only a little soft cat.

She is a small woman but not like a bird,
we are not so frail anymore,
we have become strong with bitterness,
we do not resemble any known creatures,
we are rather like young birds with extracted wings,
live cats with our fur torn out,
beasts with the living shell cracked as we drag along;
we wear a vivid nakedness that shines in the cages we have come to know.
We are no longer little singing birds.

She said,
I have papers, names and dates,
lists of women and children mutilated and beaten;
I know one child who survives.

I said,
I do not want this to be a crime of men against women,
I do not want to be afraid to put my head down,
I do not want to be afraid to have a child.
Yet I know that women do not commit such crimes
and I look at my sons with fear wondering what they do at night.

I asked,
What do we do with our knowledge
now that we have come out of innocence,
now that we have names and dates and places,
proof that the phenomenon is no longer unusual,
is not limited to that other war?

In my childhood, a boy hung a cat in a mulberry tree
and set fire to it,
he laid sand traps for anonymous creatures that could not escape

and attacked the pigeons with birdshot on Sunday afternoons.
Your father, the major, and your son-in-law
are teaching soldiers where your tender spots are,
your lover, who trained in Panama and studied in Vietnam,
arrests you in your bedroom in the middle of the night,
his caresses in the dark are for the purpose of research,
he is efficient in making you cry out.

I asked,
Now that we have names, dates and documents
relating to women and children, the dead and the dying,
what do we say to the men who lie down beside us
now that we are no longer fluttering birds,
that we are not purring kittens?
We are burned creatures with a twist in our necks
broken by the slam against the wall.

Where do we go and how do we go on
being women who resemble soft beaches,
mounds of sand dune huddled one against another,
grains of soft sand sifting into common shapes,
soft women blown by the winds,
licked by the benevolent sea
enduring for thousands of years?

I asked,
Now that we have names,
dates and documents,
evidence and warning,
do we bed down by the seas
that bear down against us?

She said,
We are no longer little singing birds.
They are pecking our eyes out,
plucking our feathers out,
eating our hearts out;
we are not soft kittens,
we are not singing birds.

Jehovah's Child

In Christ's Name, kindness is sucking the cock of a turned cheek—Jesus style—Jehovah would have bitten it off.

Straw legged Cindy,
now over the wall,
dilates prismatic eyes,
grinds unhabited wooden hips,
mousetrap cunt
with vise and swivel, just in case,
leers and extends her pay-first
scanty chocolate and strawberry nipples
to be licked from crumbling sugar cones,
a Thrifty treat—5¢ Sunday special.
She extracts from a bloody napkin dispenser,
a Volkswagen, folded mechanic and clubfooted daughter,
for entr'actes in her own private guerilla charity show,
also a ball point German shepherd with retractable pecker.
Then she mounts her own golden daughters on a
pay-as-you-go Zircon,
and is off
through the American meat grinder,
seeking enlightenment by guru in gas stations across the country,
teaching reading by billboard
and arithmetic by credit card.
$15,000 later, she races, pussy first,
through Denver, Chicago, Florida,
arrows through Seminole reservations
in a nylon cartwheel to the primitive soul,
then alligator lined, inside and out her quicksand womb,
she rolls the hospital bed out from under daddy
and wraps his heart in tin foil
for possible transplant
when her own nickel and 17 jewel version is unsprung.
Then it's New York
and tea in the tenement,
Blue Point oysters in a three fantasy walkup climbed
on reefers filched in a $2.00 trick.
In October, when burning roaches provide little heat,
she chirps a robin's going S. for winter—*Love You*—
for dough to roll into a moist and spicy
gingerbread, mink-lined, Moroccan cruise.

No takers! Pre-syphilitic, she
disconnects the 9 month telephone silence
with husband, father, god, country and all creditors at sea,
drops the mechanical spouse in the East River
with concrete daughter tied about his neck,
clamps the dog's jaw on the postman's leg
and hailing Marys on gold teeth
extracted in Catholic subway muggings,
she retreats to Convent Dolores, Dolores, Dolores.
Repentant, she reconciles testaments:
fucks only Jehovah; sucks only Christ.

The Lion of Babylon

Lion.

Yes, there were others saved,
but not my family.
When shot they fell into the ditch,
one upon the other,
for comfort on the other side.
Perhaps I passed their mass grave
on the road to Treblinka,
needing to know everything
to prepare for these last years.

Yes, others were saved once.
What price will we pay?
Soon after we met,
you became a refugee.
You were in my house
when the news came. We called
Baghdad, heard the roar of guns.
I used that word, "refugee,"
also "exile,"
but you refused them.
You could only say,
"I want to go home."

Your son says, "Please do not go home.
You will be shot." He says,
"You are a difficult woman.
You will not cover your head.
Your arms are bare in the heat.
You cannot forget you are a Professor.
You know biology.
You are stubborn," he says,
"You will not forget your studies,
that you are an expert
on the science
of all forms of life."

In your dream, possibility depends
upon offering two chickens
and a generous gift

to the beggar woman at the corner.
You have to telephone Baghdad
for the gift to be given outside the green zone.

Now only poverty protects your house,
broken windows,
all the glass on the photographs shattered
and the art collection covered in ash.
Sometimes, it seems,
you are even too depressed
to suicide in your daughter's home.

The Koran lies in the yellow dust
of a bomb crater that will carry
its own radiant light;
it will last ten thousand years.
All Merciful.
All Compassionate One.

Lion Dog sealed our fate
when she wandered
up the long hill and dared
to eat the common food,
and so the wolves attacked.
Hearing the cries,
I threw myself upon their bodies.
She ran off
but not without her wounds,
another kind of salvation.

There is a mountain lion
wandering across our land.
She left scat by the tent
where the Aleut woman was sleeping,
and has been sighted in the neighborhood.
You know as well as I do,
she is looking for water,
the water we have stolen
from all beings.

Where you lived, lions roamed once
and the Processional led to the stars.
Over Ishtar's gate it said,
"The enemy will not pass here."
Did you ever see the Lion of Babylon
amid the Hanging Gardens in your dreams?
They were one of the Seven Wonders of the World.

I also stand by helpless
when in their stead,
we offer you Shock and Awe.
Shock and Awe,
God Bless,
Shock and Awe.

Rats

The ordeal of the wounded rat
that I ordered killed,
with her family, if necessary,
by setting the guillotine,
after several years dispensation—
for not heeding the relocation order
and refusing to enter the safe transport
that had taken their relatives,
dozens upon dozens of them,
to a specially designated preserve,
a reservation, if you will.

The ordeal of the wounded rat
dragging herself across the bar
of my closet, blood flowing
onto the walls and clothes,
staining my best dresses
that had been soaked in urine
from her leafy nests
inside the chewed ceilings
and the hidden places
behind boots and skirts.

The ordeal of the wounded rat
dragging herself across the bar
of my closet, blood flowing,
her eye bulging,
from the metal shaft
that almost took her life,
when *ayin*, the eye,
is the Holy Letter
of the decade that I have entered—
Seventy.

The ordeal of the wounded rat
brought me to my knees,
as well it should do
to someone who is given the task
of being a seer,
of seeing into the past or future
for everyone, including

the rat mother, who birthed
in the skirt I wore to my son's wedding,
and hungry, ate of it,
her own holy communion.

The ordeal of the rat,
dragging herself up and down the walls,
a poor wretch nailed to a cross
and forced to carry it
up the sacred mountain
to her own death.

The ordeal of the rat,
the crucifix she carried,
the blood dripping upon
what would be her shroud;
she brought me to my knees,
that great rat mother, wounded
in the house,
on the land,
I had declared
a sanctuary for all beings.

Threnody for Camellias

And rich folks were escorted through
like tourists, with adolescent girls
staring at us while we washed like Jews
[a dozen of us naked in a shower]—
—David Ray, from "Take Me Back to Tulsa"

The one pale with age, the one who drew stings, the broken one who fell away, the discarded one, the crushed one, pressed flat as a flower between leaves of a cattle car, the one soft as stamens and humming, the one erect as pistils and unbending, the one still rosy as dawn, the streaked one and the two, one clasped on the other, are dead. All of them, in that shower, that deadly spring.

In the morning, I see the camellia collapse onto the breakfast table. Still, I say, there is meaning somewhere in the universe. Once, a shadow, sharp as the dark, pierced me, once there was something to remind me of life, once something insisted, was upright as the leaves of camellia, persisted audaciously as hardy and knobby camellia buds, never falling, never open. Once, something poignant as the bare stem of camellia, stabbed me in the heart.

This morning, the sight of the camellia holds me. A camellia entrenched against a wall cannot run, cannot escape the snip, cannot fly into the wind, can only bend. The camellia says we must refuse all miracles requiring the sacrifice of camellias. Even in the face of resurrection, we must refuse to trample the million camellias. The skies so bitterly red with camellia snow.

We cannot sweep all the millions and millions of murdered camellias into the funeral song of a single bloom. We cannot presume that the abrupt loss of this one camellia, or the happenstance prohibition of camellias, or the official refusal to issue permits for camellias, even the suicide leap of this gift of camellia, the splattered petals splayed upon a wooden table, the call to witness the camellia soul, so alert in the morning then fading from the broken flower, we can not presume this loss is as grave as the deliberate slaughter, one day, of all camellias. It isn't equatable, isn't utterable in the same breath, with the extinction of camellias, with the disappearance of the shadow of camellias in a rain that never fell, with the loss of the dream, the memory of camellias, their pale lashes, all their wide staring eyes.

The Still Point Turning Away

Everything, everything rises out of the haze or snow toward the bluebell and falls away. Seed, stem, calyx, petal, flower, fruit, rise and then all fall; seed falls, stem falls, calyx falls, petal falls, flower falls, the stalk, the dry leaf, even the dying falls away from the point of blue. The flower is long gone; the light that knew it disappears. But in the mind, that locus of the awakening of the night remains tattooed upon the memory, the way a glacier persists in the sun and grinds down whatever it rides upon.

The rain has returned. Color washes out of the trees into the ochre mud. The eucalyptus easily turns gray and the grass seeks brown. In the orchard, the remaining yellows and small oranges dull before they drop in the wind, remind me how swiftly innocent color drifts away, withdraws its inner light in this winter rain. Now it is metal that gleams; the broken white flank of the van has an eerie shimmer, the car, also aging and scratched, manages a stark, even defiant light; these sooty twin moons illuminate the day lit yard.

In the window, the astonishment of blue glass against the gray sky persists even when the mind cannot imagine anything but the drab clouds and the light, which will not hold before it, slides away. In the instance of the window, however, everything moves toward the blue, and the landscape converges in that point of sea and sky.

A photograph. Paris in the rain. A memorial. The dark bronze will last a thousand years in the dull light. A steel skeleton of the Camps grows out of barbed wire, thorn out of thorn. Spectrum of the broken light consumed at the still point where no color can exist.

Did the Beginning cohere out of night or out of day? Is it blue, which is the first color from the stars, or did the world cleave to itself out of fire and break into those yellows, reds, and oranges that wrap themselves even now about the body of wood without making any alteration of the day?

In the fireplace, wood offers another kind of light to the persistence of rain. Reading the fire, I see my people ablaze, one log, one body, against another. The more they lean, the faster they burn. Against the blackened iron, triumphant yellow flames. I have to look away to the blue glass in the window and the thin light coming through from needles of platinum stars behind the fog. I am grateful for time stretching without end beyond my own life. Those colors of fire I know too well if not firsthand. In certain countries of northern Europe, the flare of that infernal light spread like a pall, a noxious fog for years, a palette of black, red, orange, of carbon and smoke while human fat fed the bloody flames.

We saw a small lake that held light as we walked in the rain, but held it only as metal takes it on, and then the fog drifted across the hills pausing before sage, oak, gray stalks—last season's yellow mustard grass—obliterating it all.

I go to the end of the world. First color leaves. Then what? The bougainvillea, which blazed upon the fence, died back in the cold and wears the sky like a shroud. I make no predictions about what can or will endure. Birds hover silently under the brambles; even the music appears to be gone.

And I wonder about this poem. Who is it I am trying to awaken with this spectre of blue? And how? And to what?

I do not know if trees and brush drift away in fog, if they retreat from each other as we do with the coming of the dark, and as the rain lifts, remain just a little bit further apart. Safety, perhaps, only in the long run of the stars toward an impossible and necessary horizon where everything is so distant that nothing is with anything but itself. And the heart, also, fleeing in pieces, away from itself, astonished by—in awe of—the electronic spin of its parts.

"You are lonely," he said. "You are afraid." But I denied it. Pieces of broken glass are not afraid. Kindling, the gathered twigs and branches, cut logs are not afraid. I swore, "I need nothing. I want nothing I cannot give to myself. I was not, am not, will never be afraid."

Had he looked back at the pillar of salt, tincture of blue in the dying light silhouetted against the flames, corona of hell on her head, a figure of ash before the burning of cities, the mineral which she had joyously become, wouldn't he also have implored, "Let it rain," and welcomed the silence of it, cobalt rain, the blue waters, death rising, the quiet of it. Everything moving towards blue or away.

Defeats

You come home from the first battle, a bandage about the heart, grime in the palm of the hand more withered than the earth. In the ravines, the water drives mercilessly, and then the dry season leaches a great red dust. Geography in the flesh. An old folded map, tearing where it has been opened, worn, and where you've been, without knowing the four directions, the white bandage, flopping and dirty, or a gray *rebozo* bound about the breast.

When you stumble, the clay embedded in the shoes, soil of one country passing customs to another; whatever you carry—plants, meat, liquor—is forbidden. Barbed wire fences, broken glass on walls, clanging church bells and heavy iron gates against the sky, while hidden, the sacristan compels obedience with a bell rope, heavy pull of time, authority in the terrible heat, in the desire for rain, and sins, common as fleas, in the plaza.

The Hidalgo denied his mother, *La India*, but told you he went on his knees, *de rodillas*, across La Basilica de Guadalupe, "Our saint." Slow shuffling before Her. When he was young, skinned knees, stigmata, and so he pushes you onto your fours, elbows and knees, and mounts you, quivering like the lean and hungry curs. "If you have a stone," Morena said, "the dogs are stilled," as in the fearful yard, she howls the empty midnight, the astonished bitch.

In every crevice, Mexican clay, red earth, blood between the legs, menstrual and wound, the wad between the legs removed, blocked entrances to old ruins, stones pushed aside, the first invaders, thieves. Wrapped in bandages, the ancient dead cannot resist sufficiently, a pyramid between the thighs yawns reluctantly, old blood bursts out or new.

Rust stains, fire clay hardening, soil, hard packed under the plum shade, turkeys pecking the earth clean, old palm brooms sweeping. Rain carves steps in the street, and in the assault, hands, quick as machetes, husk the earth, and over all a patina of old clay disintegrating, and beneath that, shards, shattered vessels, beheaded temples, broken images, footprints, ashes. Everyone is looking for treasures, clay figurines smiling, ancient hags, *las diosas*, *la luna*, hurled out of the fire into the universe to turn about the sun.

Long after she's abandoned, the men return and find the moon dust heavy as musk. She could not keep her distance. They break the force field, the balance of nature teeters on its axis, heavy boots walk where they will over the altars of *la luna*, *las diosas*, collecting fingers, for the museum, bits and pieces, the torsos of Xochiquetzal, Xochimilco, Tlazacotl, Xipe, Coyolxauhqui, *la diosa*, *la luna*, is entered again.

Habits older than hoes honored in the resistance to fences. "Territory calling us," they say, "in her wild voice." The Hidalgo says, "Machismo is never *against* the woman," gripping his dinner knife in a fist. Where the wolves wander, chicken wire buckles before yellow eyes. In the north, the coyote, in the south, the jaguar, slither across the pelvis of the earth. It used to be, the maiden issued an invitation in the spring, her annual return. The hag, earth, grumbles, but he plows, when he plows, where he plows. *La luna* heaves, barren and powerless. He breaks into her as well, and in the battle—the bruise on your arm, did you fall? Ochre murals, red traces of sacrifices.

On the road, two volcanoes, the Sleeping Woman, Ixtacchíhuatl, and El Popo, lie in a snow sleep, inviolate through the curtained mercy of clouds. Later, one of them, *el gringo barbudo*, or the Hidalgo says, he mounted her with ropes and pitons, climbing to the very crown while Anaberta, *la bruja*, tried to scale El Popo, but, being untrained, remained at the snow line, circle of ropes, an empty epaulet upon her shoulder.

Earlier the cards say, "Danger," they say, "Beware." You say, he endangers you, that one, the American salesman, pouting *conquistadore*, pack on his back, trading new gold, new gods, *huipiles, sarapes, ponchos, rebozos, mota*. He's blond and bearded, the Huichol call him, "brother," teach him the shaman story, peyote puckers his mouth, brings dreams of Broadway, Saks Fifth Avenue, the Big Time. He says "Come, you, and Morena, the dark one, we go, we go Guatemala, we go Huatla, we go Oaxaca. Yes?" He says, "You me, the dark one, who speaks the language, she go too, she speak English, Spanish, she speak Maya, she speak Nahuatl, she speak Quiche, we go *pulque, hongos, indios, telas, mercados*. What you want? *Yerbas? Curanderos?* I buy you world."

You clutch your heart, take the spine out, *maguey* needles, the cards say "Beware," you turn your back, make a circle to call the rain, yet fearing all the elements, the way alone is better; the cliffs of Tepoztlán are sharp and steep. From the pyramid, watching like a sentinel, the owl of night hoots, *Cuidado*. You do not glance at him, his gods are daggers, lethal as old spears. *La bruja* warns, your body is in danger, you pulled the virgin card, Dona Anaberta whispers, dark eyes, the moon, *escondida* the tarot, *La Virgen*, "Don't be manhandled." A horse whinnies, Morena says, "It's the full moon." All the dogs exclaim, *Peligro*, the night undresses you, gold in the *camison* of damp and lonely sleep.

The book says: "*Los antiguos mexicanos acostumbraban sangrase casi todas las carnes del cuerpo en actos de penitencia or autosacrificio que hacien en honor de sus dioses. Utilizaban entre otros instrumentos espinas vegetales.*"

A series of openings. Altars where the hearts are torn away. As many as 10,000 a day. The sun is hungry, the heart leaps, Mexican jumping beans, grasshoppers fried in the market. "If you eat them, you'll never leave Oaxaca," the Hidalgo said. Holy locusts, chalice engraved on their backs, do god's work, eating the *milpa*, the cornfield, the corn. The land crackles with sacrifice and invaders.

The insects suck voraciously, huge welts, pyramids raised, blood suckers or bloodletting, *pulgas, chinches*. The women pack a poultice, white powder, cool cool, against the hot blood, they say "cluck cluck," cooing, the hot sun bears down, chiles burn, green and violet red, the doctor says, "The red ones, especially, are good for the heart."

The book says: "*En efecto, cinco eran los tipos de sacrificio: por extraccion del corazón, el gladiatorio, por asaeteamiento, el de fuego, y por decapitation.*"

And even earlier, before the journey, one came to her on his *norte americano* knees looking for sacrifice, begging for chains, for whipping, for her lunar mercilessness, calling her, Coyolxauhqui, *la luna diosa*, who wanted to murder her mother after a similar shame. Her heart turns over like the soil, when she turns her back, he crawls, wet and cold, into the bushes, *la culebra* cures anemia, cancer, he is colder than reptiles; there's no heat. "I will never sleep with a man I do not love," you swear, his shadow slipping toward the other snakes. She is untouched, and dances like the virgin under *la luna* which gives her no protection.

After every encounter, the women, "cluck cluck," the chickens pecking in the yard, poultices and feathers, the virgin is fifteen, *la fiesta rosa*, the blood pure and pale, we are the godmothers of the cake, frosted, like the snowy hair of Ixtacchihuatl. Pat, pat, the women make *tamales, arroz, frijoles, mole, dulce, tortillas* under the ceiling where the snakeskin hangs, *piel de culebra*, for healing, for cancer, for anemia, for blood—"*es una gran cosa para la sangre*"—and beside it, the bouquet of hot chiles, also for the heart.

Encounters in the market place, arterial chiles pulse on a white plate beside the Hidalgo, *el rubio*, from Tehuantepec where tall and strong women display peppers in pyramids to the sun. These amazons of velvet and lace teach him war, he says, calling her, "*mamita.*" He does not need a knife, nor even a flint blade, only the night and the force of arms.

To peel a chile, put it in the fire. When it blisters, pull the skin off. The flesh remains, red stains like blood, run *picante*, into the corn, the savor of the chile remains and the fire helps you toward the seeds within. Your sign is Virgo, loss surrounds you in the five colors of maize, white, yellow, speckled, blue and red.

Bougainvillaea in all colors, blood over the wall, roosters and church bells, faded dawn breaking. "On Saturday night, the men kill each other," Morena says while the women walk in the shadows. The moon hides firecrackers, shotguns, knives, quicksilver, *la culebra* in the grass. The transparent scorpion is the most deadly. The tail lunges and you're dead, you're dead, you're dead.

Her blood, the moon above, pulling your legs open, the struggle, he enters—you've never learned karate—and anyway—the knife—you haven't the strength. The snake poises, *culebra*, in the cunt, mouth, ass, biting.

You steal from the bed. What belongs to you is smeared upon the sheets, a stain you leave with him. The Hidalgo, *conquistadore*, turns to press against the bloodroot, whispers, "*Te amo. Tu eres una mujer fabulosa.*"

Later, she falls running down the streets broken from so much water, steps down, or up, from the altar where the knife cut the heart out, the sun has to eat, heat, heat. The moon is hiding, you scrape against the wall, dogs sleep under collapsed bougainvillaea, chiles explode out of their dark skins, blood between her legs, terra cotta pottery, shattered figures buried and unearthed.

Red chiles, *grandes y pequenos*, red and rust colored scorpion tailed *huipiles*, red rust, blood colored *rebozos, chile salsa, mole*, peppers ground fine, red powder on fingers, the flaming cockscomb crowing, the red fire rising.

The women go, "cluck cluck," they rub her body with oil, anti-venom, a poultice. They wash her, the *temezscal* woman beats her with *zapote* leaves against *los aires*. Your back is cold like the moon, the hags beat you till the steam rises, a mist against the sun, nothing can be seen of the Sleeping Woman. Sweat on her breast beading, vapors rising, her skin rubbed clean, shining like the moon. Waters silver the night, the flood running clear, you can drink it, the well is good. The chickens peck the garden clean, the turkey hens gobbling the refuse, the cock preening his feathers, the red comb, like blood, falling between her legs.

The egg is full of poison. The yolk is buried. Her heart is beating beating. They pack a poultice of white clay, a seal, the kiln, the fire, the hard pottery, the goddess, *la diosa, la luna*, the laughing figurines. Flowers sweep over the walls. She is named Xochil, flower.

The rains come. Mud flows, blood, over the houses of the *conquistadores*. You come home. The women go "cluck cluck," they spin about you, little white eggs, they break open clean, the stream is white, the maize is yellow, the *zapote* leaves are fresh, new trees over old ruins. The old women grin, pat, pat, *tortillas, tamales* wrapped carefully as bandages, *acostarte acostarte*, go to sleep, go to sleep, a gray *rebozo* binds her breast, a hammock hanging from the horns of the stark moon.

Because So Much New Way of Being

It was a night for listening to Corelli, Geminiani
Or Manfredini. The tables had been set with beautiful white cloths
And bouquets of flowers. Outside the big glass windows
The rain drilled mercilessly into the rock garden, which made light
Of the whole thing. Both business and entertainment waited
With parted lips, because so much new way of being
With one's emotion and keeping track of it at the same time
Had been silently expressed. Even the waiters were happy.
—John Ashbery, from "Someone You Have Seen Before"

> The shell consisted of approximately 8,000 half gram flechettes, these arranged
> in five tiers, a time fuse, body shearing detonators, central flash tube, smokeless
> propellant charge with a dye marker contained in the base and tracer element.
> The functioning of the shell was as follows; the time fuse fires, flash sent down
> the flash tube, shearing detonators fire, and the forward body splits into four
> pieces, body and first four tiers dispersed by the projectile's spin, last tier and
> visual marker by the powder charge. The flechettes spread, mainly due to spin
> . . . in an ever widening cone along the projectile's previous trajectory prior to
> burst. The round is a highly effective anti-personnel weapon—soldiers report
> that after beehive rounds were fired during an over-run attack, many enemy
> dead had their hands nailed to the wooden stocks of their rifles, and these dead
> could be dragged to mass graves by the rifle. . . . It is said that the name beehive
> was given to the . . . [weapon] due to the noise of the flechettes moving
> through the air resembling that of a swam of angry bees.
> —Wikipedia Shrapnel (Vietnam era)

On one side of the big glass windows the table is set with beautiful white cloths, bone china,
one would think, and fresh flowers, but it is only one side of the big glass windows. On the
other side, the big glass windows are one barrier to the light between worlds. Here we are in
the driving rain. Blinded. Or among the angered bees, buzzing. No birthday here, despite
the celebration on the one side. It's a death day on this other side, like everyday, don't you
think, death day like any other? The light coming from the rock garden is the friction of
pickaxes or shovels against stone. The rocks don't want to be here. They had other lives
before us among their own.

Outside the big glass window there is no living language for the world within the room of
big glass windows, no language to speak of for what that room has become. It isn't creation,
after all, inside, exactly, because

". . . we are a part of it and
Can live in it as in fact we have done
Only leaving our minds bare for questioning
We now see will not take place at random
But in an orderly way that means to menace
Nobody—the normal way things are done."[19]

Here in the redemption of the driving rain are the white cloths of surrender to something beyond ourselves. We wrap ourselves in them, shrouds of the old life that we pray has been taken away, not buried, but taken where we might avoid contaminating the soil or soul further. Recycle the poison. Transform the exquisite gourmet menu to something robust that can reproduce itself, that isn't limited to this one lifetime on your translucent bone plate, a meal that has a lineage and a future. Don't we have the technology yet? About radiation, they say, no problem, or we can take it out to sea or . . . if we finish the sentence as politely as one does at a dinner party where everything is possible because it is spoken we will have chosen sides, as

". . . each moment
of utterance is the true one; likewise none is true."[20]

we will have shaped language, even a poem into a weapon, but can it, really, as it appears, penetrate the haze, our breath, our trespasses, piercing as shrapnel or shell fragments do or sometimes as only DU can buzz, breach tanks, flesh, earth.

It was not transparent, despite the big glass windows, that the tables had been set to be viewed by someone passing who can't come in but might want to, being wet and in the dark despite the rock garden;

". . . anybody who doubts that need only look out of the window
Past his or her own reflection, to the bright, patterned,
Timeless unofficial truth hanging around out there."[21]

That truth, the passing beggar, homeless, the exiled, the refugee, ex-combatant, child soldier, the waiter's kid without a babysitter, might want also to be noted in the manner of those who are eating, by name and worldly assignment. Gilt by association.

Here on the other side there is no glass between inside and outside and the tables are just cloths on the earth. Somewhere, the *lappa*, the *kanga*, the *iro*, the *kitenge*, the *kikoy*, the printed cloth a woman wears as a skirt, or to bind a baby to her, to sit on, or to serve food. The kids are with her wherever she is, at work or at home or in the field, why not, we are all part of the same life, are we not?

---

19   "Self-Portrait in a Convex Mirror," John Ashbery.
20   Ibid.
21   "Someone You Have Seen Before," John Ashbery.

When they had reached the end of their endurance, the women of Liberia sat down on their *lappas* in the horrific heat and the torrential rain and wouldn't move, dawn to sundown, until the war was over. We brought them plastic bottles of water as they had no money even to buy drinks, while they repeated, "Give us your guns, please." In return, the child soldiers got a bag of rice—and enough money for drugs for a few months—our wars had addicted them against their will—then they were on the lam again. The women's cloths are not white but printed in the colors of mud, cattle or leopard, sometimes sky and lake with an arrangement of brown tipped whispering reeds, or an arraignment of ducks in a row, decoys, or the red scars on the feathered cheeks of the red faced cordon-bleu.

I want to avoid blood colors here, hoping only for scarlet in feathers, berries, flowers, roses, orchids, weavings, women's adornment, beads, but something crimson is dripping down her legs right onto, damn it, the white tablecloth. What do you think it is? Death, probably. Don't you think? Death is inside her or upon her body, scratching more than the surface. This is the truth: If someone doesn't want to know, then the poem becomes an ornament, like a party favor or flowers cut down in their youth flown from Israel, Kenya, India, or Columbia to Holland and then to your table. Or direct without rendition. Fragile exiles, refugees, or prisoners, waiting for relocation. A single sentence can embellish the past that isn't coming to an end quickly enough, and why would one choose a poem to speak about this when the poem is speakeasy and has been for decades.

Where is the poem that can say what needs to be said? What are we bringing to the table? Is it important to write a poem, is it important, still, if the deadly life is half-life enough to give a big tip to the happy waiter whose father or mother or sister or brother or child, god help us, was shot or beaten or thrown down from one of our vehicles, helicopters, or as the testifying soldier said, "They used to hover so low, it took a lot of skill and steel nerves to buzz and behead the farmers in their fields and rice paddies, how close could you get, how sharp." There is nowhere, nowhere for him, the waiter or perhaps her if the joint isn't too elegant, the waitress, nowhere, to make a living, no way, there is no living, but waiting, happy, happy waiters, happy time, waiting to gain a few bucks, going down in value every time he or she understands what he or she is doing, serving beer fattened veal or pâté de foie gras, also stuck down the throat, waterboarding the animals, so he can, she can eat what the maître d' decides is left over enough to feed the help, or scrape the plates, surreptitiously, into a doggie bag for the kids. Help! Help!

Can the poem be accurate as a bullet? Can we kill with it, one or many, shrapnel, or simply stun, stop someone long enough, you, reader, hey, listen, help, do something, someone is dying. Who? Are you afraid it's you? No, can't be. It's a kid. It's only a kid. He raised his rifle, the soldier said after his breakdown, that is how you do things in Baghdad, and he said, he couldn't wait, he said, to see who that curly head belonged to. By the time it raised sufficiently, he would have been caught in those other gun sights, you never know, and you have to protect yourself. But guess what, surprise! it was a kid hiding there that he had just blown away. It could be yours, your kid, he could have, he looked just like you, the soldier said. Could have been. . . . Not a chance, you say, your kids are safe, you make sure of it, that's what this war is about, isn't it? Thanks buddy, for helping us out.

Help. Listen. Where is the language that will strike you in the heart? The boy we met, those boys, and then the woman, probably too, the one we call her Mama, as she is Mama to the boys, several boys, girls ex-combatants, child soldiers, men, two generals, have eaten human hearts for its manna. "You're eating my heart out," my mother used to say when I was wild with grief, with lust, with joy, or merely with adventure. Now we have to bring them back to us, rock them in our arms so that the killing fields that we have plowed and planted with so many white bones will not expand to become other forests running red or other deserts of radiant metal. These ones, we captured to do our deeds, they were our children once, and become so again, in our arms. Everyone has had a mother. Everyone is a motherless child. We are their mothers again. "Ai la lu, oh ai la lu, my baby. In your momma's arms lie weeping. And soon you'll be a sleeping bird, so ai la ai la ai la luuuuu."

That white tablecloth. That shroud. Its stain is irreversible. Nothing will clean these little hands. Not all the perfumes of Arabia, the stench of Baghdad. How do you like your meat done? Charred but bloody? Those meals we longed for, white linen tablecloths, sterling silver, crystal, bone china from the bone business,[22] bone wagons, bone roads, half a million tons of buffalo bones were shipped from Texas alone to grace your dinner table, so we can eat whatever we want before the open window where the rain is not falling any longer onto the earth, the dry bonescape is everywhere.

One truly broken heart is all the lonely God needs to weep.

---

22   "Bone Business," The Handbook of Texas Online,
http://www.tshaonline.org/handbook/online/articles/BB/dxb3.html.

Pelicans in the East

If there are four suits,
and the first is East, Air,
birds associated with the dawn,
fine eyes that see
where the blue, lake or sea
meets the green or sand,
we think this kind of vision,
has something to do with wisdom,
at least that is what the augury implies,
or the ones who still remember
to bless and invoke the four directions,
beginning with air and wind,
those invisible intelligences
that are called *Beginning* and *Mind*.

What do we say then of the deaths
of eight thousand baby pelicans,
whose mothers could not rip
open their own bodies—
as they are said to do—
to save them?
Last year, and this year again,
the mothers and the fathers
tried sudden and mysterious flights,
thousands of them also,
to parts unknown.

This year the chicks have succumbed.
to what? We don't know, we say,
but let's call it West Nile disease
because the Nile is far away
and its waters are said to serve our enemies,
and because we do not want to know
the death we carry in each breath.

I could go on to search out the deadly ways
imposed on each direction, the ways
Water from the West serving our dreams,
the deep place where the unknown generates
its occult wonders and the water spirits,
sprightly and magical,

has become the toxic womb of demented whales
beaching themselves on uranium-yellow sands
of the South.

Or the way Fire from the South has been set loose,
ancient beasts going up in smoke,
just as our modern fairy tales depict it:
The prehistoric monster shaking itself loose
by earthquake and flying in a whirlwind
called cyclone or tornado or hurricane.
Then in a later transformation
befitting a fire-breathing dragon,
it sets the forest alight.
In this direction is the heart of the world:
see how enflamed it has become.

What's left? Ah, yes, Earth,
the North, from this perspective,
where the icecap is melting,
the ocean rising, already islands
going the way of Atlantis,
tsunamis breeding in the deep,
and everywhere elephants,
tigers, wolves, squirrels,
creatures of every sort, expiring.
The tundra itself will soon be littered
with the corpses of polar bears,
seals, walruses and all manner of
great sea animals and fish.
Earth, the North, manifestation,
The Great Mother, the prima materia,
your body, everything that matters,
dematerializing in our hands.

Why do I tell you this? You know it all.
It is too much to bear for anyone or any being,
and so the pelican mother,
reputed to open the veins of her body
when her chicks are hungry and there is no food,
didn't. Couldn't. The ground was not covered
with her bloody feathers. Traumatized

we lose our way, our instincts and wisdom.
The air was heavy
with the tiny cries of her little ones,
one note of an infant flute,
an exact trill of anguish.

Multiply it now, a thousand times.
Listen. Two thousand. More. Eight thousand.
The little ones surprised
to see themselves dying,
all of them so soon after their birth.
This wasn't the world they were promised
in the egg.

Pelicans in the Midwest

The chicks died. Eight thousands of them. And you almost died too. You may be breaking the way so many fragile eggs broke, vulnerable as the bird nation to the poisons that erode the essential structures of our lives.

It is not enough to grieve, but to know this grief, its cause, its devastation, its imponderable effects upon everything it touches. We make a poison and cannot control its spread. It is a power with a mind of its own. It wants to be itself, and everything it touches dies, quickly in some cases, or over long, long stretches of time, a human lifetime, or longer, we do not know. And those, like yourself, who never made the poison, who stand against it, who cast a sacred circle to protect what is inside, who become the trees against an ill wind, still succumb. We can't protect the circle and the wind wasn't asked where to carry the powder. It wasn't asked where to set it down, or how to free itself from what it would never take up on its own.

What is the choice? To take the grief into ourselves, or to take the poison into ourselves, or both, on this terrible path we are asked to carve toward a different kind of knowledge than the kind we have been taught to gather to us and to call power. Knowledge is power, we were told.

This is not power. Look how the white powder has made a powder of our bones. Look how the egg dissolves at the slightest tremor. Look how it cannot protect or sustain what it loves.

I try to write this and I have only music to offer. A certain music in the rhythm or the arrangement of words alongside each other so that they become companions to a vision too far away to see. We do not know *and* it depends entirely on us. And then the song I never knew before takes me and I hear the words I don't know to speak:

The challenge is to become the pelican though we have never entered the territory of pelican mind. Grief is the shimmering cry that can bind us to each other so exactly that there will be no distinction between one thought, one being, and another, the way the pelicans glide together upon the lower breezes and currents in graceful lines that simultaneously display their acquiescence and their intent.

Like the pelican, we look down at our chicks and watch them die. We observe helplessly—that is our calling. If we pretend for a moment that there is something we can do, we will have lost contact with pelican mind. Making this connection, difficult as it may seem, is what we can do. So then let us observe hopelessly as they must do. You—I—we must do this. We must be helpless for a long time and then, afterwards, when we pick up our lives, we will not pick up anything at all that will do harm. We will not weigh one harm against another, or one creature, or one species. We will not choose the immediate over the long run or this moment over the future. We will not choose the lesser of two evils; we will not be expedient or resigned. We will not.

Such a garment of sorrow you are asked to wear. Such a delicate silk woven from your own body, your own tears, from a storm of feathers. A strange raiment that will never be a fashion. Yet, clad this way, you will do everything for these little ones, our beloveds, your chicks, your babes, now flesh of your flesh. Yes, your babes, their little lives, your little ones, your own body, your little life, all our little lives.

When Paradise Is Not

I thought it was the morning of the birds. The first constellations of water fowl landing before the dawn and then a lone hippo silhouetted in the yellow field before he entered the pan and submerged himself.

We set out and came, at the end of our foray, to the pan where the hippo was heading, where his small family waits under water. Between this moment and the first moment there was nothing.

You could see where the elephants had been in the night, their huge feet pressing mud into the shape of their bodies so they would remember. Two crowned cranes rose black and white, magnificent, and flew to the other side of the water. One could think or hope we were witnessing original chaos leading to creation but this was not the vision we had been awakened for.

This is not the ark. This is not preservation or salvation. Only desolation and nothingness. No game. No animals. No brothers or sisters. No wisdom or intelligence. No movement or beauty between one pan and the other except for the hardy yellow horny bird and an occasional invisible peeper. Otherwise the palate is dry and the symphony silent.

This is the end. We have crossed the world to see it when we hoped to be graced with visions teeming with life and color so that our own small pains might be relieved.

Dear sweet God. *Tatenda*, Thank you, for this vision of the endless suffering we have wrought.

I had spent days in Chobe watching large herds of elephants roll in the mud, submerging themselves and emerging with the dark wet earth covering their bodies with the source of beginnings.

Between the waters of Chobe and the dry heat of Hwange are barriers of concrete and obstacles of cities and barbed wire obstructions of corporate farms. The work of creation has come to an end.

We saw this. We saw the dark shapes disappear in the white dawn. We saw that there had been many and now there were few. An eagle circled the pan unraveling a spiral of DNA over the trees at the edge of the white termite mound. No one came to stir the waters.

We pray that the animals will return this afternoon to grace us with their small numbers so we can forget this terrible vision of the future with which the Divine has graced us so. We will think we were simply unlucky. We will blame something or someone outside ourselves.

But, truly, we see it all . . . life teeming and life exterminated. So we pray. It is all beyond us. Not death, that is so easy, but life. We seem incapable of serving it.

We want to live apart. We do not want to work with our hands. We do not love mud. We do not praise it. How then do we imagine creation?

River of Light

A Lake in the Mind

What's essential is a lake in the mind,
and then this wind freshening, blowing through the windows, insistent with the assurance of
morning,
but now the shimmer of the first moon
on the waters and the blue glimmer of the night sky alive with invisible stars

and such a long draught of silence—
the water clear and coming from a source
which is either
at the very core of the earth
or somewhere far beyond earth in the heavens—
that we speak of it in the only language we know,

the early morning or midnight of the lake, the first streak of birdsong
across the waters, the way the moonlight breaks,

this language, being the only language for what it is we wish to speak about without saying a
word,

the early morning or midnight of the lake and the first streak of birdsong
and
the wind blowing across the surface of the mind like a bell.

The Burning Bush

On a wintering tree,
the astonishment of light.
The Burning Bush is everywhere.

The Cold Sun

Perhaps it happens this way in every universe, separation leading toward gradual cooling, the cells of the body beginning to pull apart from each other, the fierce, clutching mammalian heat that quenches itself in engendering, easing, and everything going its chilly way. Mars loosed and Venus certainly. Afterwards, Earth, Andromeda, Pisces, the Swan, the Snow Bird, set out determinedly toward distance. Old ones, at their end, climbing to the top of the mountain or set out on the ice. The last country is the cold country where each atom, each particle, is finally free.

The wise ones say: "Don't hold on." They say, "With an open palm." The temperature drops. Zero centigrade. Nirvana and rapture. Light stretching languidly into a slow red glow, wave after gentle wave toward the inevitable finish that is blue for the ice of it.

The confusion of color is temporarily engaging: the sunset of blue, the old sun cooling but turning red, the coming night of separation, and the intermittent peeps of those who have gone before us, a falsetto of wisdom blown apart. Blizzard, storm, hail, fog, then only that hazy trail of dust upon which we step and lighten, step and lighten and then dissolve.

The leaf looses itself, takes on a disguise, wraps itself in a cloak of a warmer color to set out alone. Youth calls this loneliness.

What are you doing? We are making time. We are making time in the vast distances between words. In the great snowy silences of white unfolding into white.

I thought I should go to the pole for the elongation of dark, the endless night, but it is not time yet. In another decade or two when my own rhythms match a day, dark weeks long, and an equally unhurried midnight. Just the faintest and most polite interruption of sunrise and sunset. A glow only before the stars return.

By then I will have learned to write by hand, so that each word is shaped and deliberate, each word itself, fashioned as if it were a rare stone, a gift of a piece of wood, the sacrifice of a life offering itself to the gesture of a knife that calls it forth. The more remote path is the space between the words. Not to leave monuments, not to litter the landscape with what has been said and will be eternally unmoving and fixed, but the effort to bring the word to its own shape exactly before it goes its own way. The two of us, but not ever again, the rub of body and mind against body and mind, hand in hand.

The old people teach us to hunt extremity, to set out after the beast that will not be brought back and that will. To hunt the bear and be the bear. You follow the hunger that is only sated by thirst and so wants nothing. You must go miles toward every horizon with nothing between you and the absolute circle that marks the end of the worlds.

Without practice and without preparation. There can be no rehearsals for every step is a step, every path is a path, every direction is a direction, every way is a way. No going back, no beginning again. The setting out is the setting out. And no one will return who has ever tasted the sweet snow, the intangible and exquisite blue, the solitary and endless rapture of the long cold night spaces in between.

Crazy Old Woman

Crazy old woman,
screaming at her flock,
chases us across
the dry river
to Paradise.

The Mouth of the River

At the mouth of the river of light
streaming into phosphorescent breakers,
one can drown, but
the wolf was ecstatic in the weaving of the tides.
The heron was not a branch heavy with barnacles,
nor a metal pole marking the entrance to the sea,
nor a warning for swimmers or boats,
but her own blue self stilling the waves.
When the wolf came close, she rose,
soaring,
into the sky.

They say, one can drown
even at the mouth of the river of light.
It would not be such a bad death to go down
in the luminous surge
of tiny night creatures.

I Drank the Silence of God Out of the Stream in the Trees[23]

God has no measure. In the certain moment of this utterance, whatever is meant falls away. Still the mind goes out like a surveyor in the morning, scaling the hills and dividing one parcel from another, establishing fence posts. Each day of knowing something substantial, each conviction, each clear understanding of the nature of beginnings and endings, each new definition and distinction, prokaryote, eukaryote, quark, proton, molecule, species, genus, family, order, phyla, is precipitated out from knowing, falls away, like a suit of clothes, like a cocoon, a shell, a brown leaf, like an old skin. Is not recovered.

God is elsewhere. And without measure. Not immeasurable but outside of measure. In the garden perhaps. In the free and immoderate twisting of the olive tree toward the light, in the lake exhorting the rain, the nestling of stones into earth, the unexplainable intimacy of time folding against the shoulder of death.

Imagine the two lovers, this world and the other world. I sequester myself in the crease between their arms enfolding each other. Each with its own sweat and breath. The scent of the living and the perfume of the dead.

Small enough to be invisible between them, I lean into the stride of one and then the other. The long glide as on black ice in one direction and the other. To the east, to the west. To the north, to the south. From the center to infinity.

An aura from the commingling of the two, as of yellow sulphur in a white mist pulsing out of the center of the earth. Without the hand of earth, no center.

Not sitting lightly upon, not within, not outside of, not evident and not hidden, a separate category without category, for not absent either anywhere, and not present. The Egyptian God Thoth weighs the heart after death. Against a feather of light. For its heaviness or for its lightness? For its matter or its spirit? For its joy or for its grief?

Descend the stairs. Come into the chamber of the god with your heart in your hand. Offer up your life. There. Only some odd particles moving at the speed of light. Glimmers to ignite the divine hand.

---

23   Title from *De Profundis*, George Trakl, translated from the German by James Wright.

Stumbling along the forest path, night falling like boulders, the firefly illuminated the way, then it vanished. The stars do not form an abacus. The light passes through us. We disappear as well.

If I Had Not Climbed Mt. Sinai, I Would Not Know North

God of the extreme moment,
ecstasy of fierce beauty,
gray, luminous circles of birds,
holy letters of bone,
trees splayed onto snow,
in versions of the sacred name,
we do not know if we will
melt or freeze in the vapors
of the stars
only that we vanish
in the Presence.

But first
the heart
is split open

    YA

and then quartered

    VA

The River Does Not Turn on Itself

The sieve asks
to marry the river.
The spirits say,
the river belongs to the bank,
say, this old earth
knows how to move along
the shoulder of water
without loss.
The jug takes the river
to her mouth;
she has lived through fire
and cooled in leaves.

The river goes
where it must,
it cannot linger
in these bare hands.
Spirits follow
the river,
and the drawer of water
fashions her bucket
from bone.

Make Me a Vessel for Your Light

We spend a lifetime preparing a vessel, then another soul, who has had the pottery of his face or her eye shattered by inevitable circumstance, hears the call and knows each body's sacred chalice has room enough for legions of dead. And so lands.

Shamans in the mountains of Peru provoke spirits into song by blowing into clay jugs.

The new voice resembles the tonal singing of Tibetan monks in the Himalayas who have found that by chanting for hours and together, they sing several octaves at once.

Some months ago as I was turning toward another dimension, I held the wing of an owl aloft as if participating in a ceremony and because my eyes were closed, I felt the full weight of the once living owl alight and enter the wing. Also, then, the smoke of owl spirit making light of the matter.

Here then is the messiah. A suspension bridge across time asking for goodness between us.

Language extended so far it touches us at the same moment, though one may be sleeping and the other awake. Time in its infinite compassion, cradling everything equally, past, present, future, bringing the dead into that warm niche under our arms to enact an embrace.

No wisdom is lost. It all curls back into song. Phantom octaves open there, in the heart beyond us.

In this moment, no despair.

Thus It Is Written

In Homage, Tehuti

The God of Death
was the God of all words,
and the God of all that heals,
and of everything built,
and of the stars.

This God of Death
was born a man or a woman
and inscribed his teachings
on an emerald,
but when they were found
they were in the form of a heart
and the heart was the color blue
that inspires us to say
lapis lazuli
in its presence.

It is said that
the daughters of ice,
one blue and one green,
meeting
at the base of a glacier,
are the rivers of God.

They do not mix
when they go to the sea,
but in salt
they become the mother
of all creatures
who takes them in equally.

How do we know this?

The God of Death
wrote it on water
and we drink it.

This potion is called words.
Our body is made of this.

On our death
we will run
back to God
as a waterfall.

Thus it is written.

The Well

At the bottom of the well,
where the moon snake
suckles her tail,
is the universe of stars.
The narrow dark
leading to the water
cloisters itself
against the broad stream of day,
until, at the furthest point
the blue sky fades
into mother night
and all the milky points
of light begin
the long descent home
to underground seas.

The ancients knew this.
They set their secret ziggurats
in the earth's core,
clambering down the night shaft
of day to drink the stellar vision
that even the sun
cannot extinguish,
and after nights
and nights of daylight
ascended with the sign
of the heavenly sparks
in their luminous eyes.

You Come to Me in Light

You come to me
through Light,
from the beginning,
the luminous one
at the foot of my crib.

Now in golden purple,
as if a sunset
in the bare tree,
as if the fire inside
were manifest,
       and Beauty everywhere.

A Love Letter to God

This is the anniversary of my father's death. My father died ten years ago with the Sh'ma, sweet in his mouth. Honey of a Promised Land leading him forward. And all the grief and joy of having lived so long behind him.

What caused my father acute pain in his dying was a plastic container taped to his penis so that he wouldn't wet his bed. His weak hands twitched over the sheets attempting to remove it until I asked the nurse to do what I couldn't do.

As he was dying, the Challenger exploded.

After the nurse left, I covered my father's hand on the bedrail with my own and spoke my love for him. It was some hours after midnight and I was weary having flown that evening from Ohio to his bedside. I gently disentangled my hands from his and lay down next to him on another bed. Within the hour he died.

On a day when the Bal Shem Tov couldn't pray, he searched for a man with a broken heart to open the gates of heaven. Unsuccessful in his quest, he found a man whose heart he broke. "You are a fraud," he screamed at the astonished rabbi of the humble synagogue where they had just said the morning prayers. "None of your prayers have ever been sincere. Now pray."

He did and the gates of heaven opened.

When I began this letter, my heart was broken, but not sufficiently. But after a few hours of prayer I felt for an instant the great heartbreak of God.

When my father was a little boy, God stopped him on his way to school and said, "You are my beloved." From then on, my father knew God's sorrow.

As I write this, the garden is full of birds, doves burst into the air like buds opening everywhere at once: God, in Your forms of Beauty, be with me.

Spring comes in the heart of winter. One season enfolding into the other. A blooming acacia fell over the night of my friend's death, seven days into the new year. The roots ripped out of the soil like a grave's bones catapulted into the air during an earthquake. We raised it up again. For years, it burst into yellow flowers to mark her death, then it fell again and died this time, even as she died, and lived among us, and then, ultimately, died away from us.

The rains come, the temperature falls, and the birds return. Quail hurry across the ground as red and yellow-breasted finches gather at the feeder. Jasmine leaps to the bare elm, winds about the naked branches, green and flowering. The daring crimson of bougainvillea flares up among the same green branches. By the time I die the tree will be a winter blaze of red, purple and orange. That fire will keep us warm.

The leafless pomegranate tree bears burnished red husks, hollow bells browning along the cracks where they burst open and are pecked empty by birds. The first thin stalks of a pepper tree have rooted themselves in the heart of the pomegranate that was alone on the hill for almost twenty years. This pubescent girl of a pepper is waving her Japanese fan of small red berries. Spring and winter as delicate and fleeting as cherry blossoms.

The wild jungle that wisteria weaves, her delicate blossoms hiding the stranglehold of vine tying the trees into a single noose. All the trees stand together or all the trees fall down.

⁓

Now on the top of the telephone pole a living Tlingit mask—red head, black cheeks, black collar, speckled breast, black beak, some small deity surveying his landscape. Flicker. The rain bird of the Chumash has come home. He turns displaying the perfect geometry of his triangular red cap, the brown and black stripes on the wings, white lightning flashing down his spine into the black of his tail.

⁓

This is the task: Learn the secret languages of light again. Also the letters of the dark. Learn the flight patterns of birds, the syllables of wolf howl and birdsong, the moving pantomime of branch and leaf, valleys and peaks of whale calls, the long sentences of ants moving in unison, the combination and recombination of clouds, the codices of stars. Thus reconstitute the world sign by sign and melody by melody.

Here comes a gang of crows. I didn't realize I was longing for the dark.

⁓

When I was eight, my father was fifty-four. Four men carried him home after he fainted in the subway. He was laid out, simultaneously bier and corpse. I don't know why they didn't climb the seven steps of the stone stoop to the front of the door but instead came around the side, twisting to the left up the two stairs of the dark entrance way, twisting to the right up three steps, twisting to the left again when the door was opened to enter the narrow hallway and lay my father down on the couch in the living room. These pallbearers were angels, of course. They disappeared immediately. My father awakened and looked at my mother with two words on his mouth: "The war."

Not knowing what to do, my mother made him eat a bowl of soup. She asked him to fix the bathroom drain and weed the garden. She contrived numerous tasks and errands for him. When he completed one, she devised another. Secretly, at night, he remembered what had brought him to his knees

If we can't bear it, what we can say about God?

⁓

This is what I know: God is not steel or any of the indestructible alloys we have created. God is sandstone stretching up from deep in the earth to the roof of the sky. God is the same stone etched by two white rivulets we call current and waterfall, flowing endlessly, sweet and salt, carving the right and left hands whose names are also beauty and sorrow, so that every drop rives the four chambers of the great heart. This is eternal. The rising and the falling. The bitter and sugary. The burn and the poultice. Division and communion. It never ceases: dismay and hope, agony and forgiveness. These are the four directions that sun and moon mark for us and that day and night illuminate. This is what we call east, north, south, west, thinking we can walk one way or another and not succumb to windstorm, earthquake, volcano and drowning.

We want to be God in all the ways that are not the ways of God, in what we hope is indestructible or unmoving. But God is the most fragile, a bare smear of pollen, that scatter of yellow dust from the tree that tumbled over in the storm of my grief and planted itself again. God is the death agony of the frog that cannot find water in the time of the drought we created. God is the scream of the rabbit caught in the fires we set. God is the One whose eyes never close and who hears everything.

⁓

I saw God in a whirlwind illuminated by the solstice fires of northern lights. God was a great black bird, longer than time, flying across the holy letters calling out the dying of the year and a new beginning. So I gave myself as a handmaiden who would like nothing but to bring comfort, warm wine and spices, to the broken heart of her beloved, just as it was my father's way to soothe his young daughter's grief with glasses of warm milk, sweetened with honey.

⁓

This is the day of my father's death. The birds are everywhere. Funeral wreaths of clouds and bouquets of twitters and feathers. This is the anniversary of my father's death. This is the day of loss and remembering. This is the anniversary of my father's death. I awakened heart broken and full of prayer. Nothing can be fixed, but what reconstitutes me is a vision through a pinhole in time and space of the lonely God carrying the burden of universal sorrow. I want to take Her in my arms. I want to stroke His temples.

But God does not have a body and so my hands cannot ease Her. Sing with me, then, the Song of Sorrow.

Ruin and Beauty

Ruin and Beauty

Ruin had never been in the forest where Beauty lived until the bear offered himself in marriage to the girl. Like the unicorn trapped by innocence and woven into an eternal tapestry of silken threads, he lost his life, and all his lives to follow, to what she thought she desired: to be free of his unexpected appearances where she was picking berries, and her pail not quite full yet, or to lie on his thick fur but only after it was skinned from his body, or even, when she was hungry, to eat his flesh; but not to walk the same trails, century after century, in the cautious companionship and sweet distance that would have given them each their true lives. That is the kind of wife an innocent girl becomes.

Beauty is the name she is given in the fairy tales, but truly she is Ruin. Beauty belongs to the forest and the forest dwellers and the stones. Ruin belongs to the girl and her brothers, her father and mother, and her sons who came also from Beauty but have forgotten their father.

After the death of Beauty by the brothers and sons, everything we do justifies Ruin. Everyone says it is inevitable, says it has always been among us, says it is the way things are and must be. Everything must come to Ruin. It used to be that a man would only ruin a woman; that, the bear could never do. But now the ruin of fingerprints is on the skin of everything that is or ever was.

Ruin goes where humans go, our inseparable twin, our shadow. Ruin was never within the desert where all life is finely polished to sand, or of the forest where even the dead trunk stripped of everything over years remains a thing of beauty. Here is a fallen log that lightning has splayed open, crown to root. Lying by the lake in a bed of leaves among banners of yellow straw, it has become a boat to carry vision.

These lives we have made are not lives. Each being, other than ourselves, awakens each morning into itself and dies there too.

The wild turkey, that stupid bird, appeared from within the forest within an hour to accept my offering of scattered corn, and left me a feather as a boundary stone where our two realms had agreed to merge.

At the end of the day when two ravens announced the coming storm, Lady Turkey raised her head. While the others continued to scavenge, she listened. Listened, without scampering. Without raising her feathers in alarm. Listened to the sly language spoken out of our hearing by the remaining speakers, those who have not yet been put to death. When the others had eaten their fill or left something for today, and the rain began falling, she followed them, thoughtfully, we can say.

The bear left me his signature and in return I left him blueberries. I did not hunt him down. The next day, Beauty left a rune upon the birch, a sign in an ancient language our people used to speak that means, Our Common Fate.

In my dreams, we wander together in the luminous graveyard of stars. There nothing I know does harm and my innocence is not a snare. Beauty speaks in the ways that I dream, in the ways I have always known.

In the day, I sit on the stump that Bear raked with his claws to tell me he's near. When I am certain that we are entirely alone, I ask: Where is our dead language buried? How can we disinter its bones?

Setting Out

Your birth sign:
"Receptive."
You are always
opening doors.

This drum,
a slit trunk,
once called through all the trees,
sounds never heard
in a house.

Hunters and gatherers knew
all the animal languages.

Now even the whisper
of corn
fades
in the opposing wind.

Star Walk

Walking at night under the remaining stars. Something lethal stirring the scent of dry sage and early narcissus. Something slightly chemical chafing the odor of the turned earth and the snorting horses. The night wind slithers through the gully, cold and sharp, a momentary freshening.

Outside the rare realm of leaves and bare earth, thoughts both metallic and mechanical rasp through the mind like a chainsaw, cutting small pieces into smaller pieces. The dreams disappear, not even as fallen leaves, but as leaves that have failed to sprout, like the yolk of the poisoned egg that will never be a bird. The disappearance of the unborn. What might have been. Unbearable.

Danger everywhere, signs and portents, miracles and catastrophes. The hammer of one ambition against another, fusion and fission. And then an unending firestorm in the mind. Enter the grim reaper of the death of spirit. Alarmed, I put my hand into the poultice of earth.

At my feet, a wild trapezoid of new grace, her legs angling away from her body in a stretch of memory holding snow, the midnight sun, the blue continuous night in her paws, and despite that radiance, Isis, the great white wolf of the Arctic, is helpless against the disappearance of the time before, the time before, the time before, endless time disappearing.

To walk into the unknown to make it known may not be the way. To open the door underground and pass through, flooding it with Herculean light, may not be the way. To streak in a straight line into the sky, trail of gases blazing, may not be the way. Traveling forward in a straight line to the end of the universe without looking back, afraid even of the opalescent curve at the end of the shell of time, may not be the way.

Where is the smaller circle that cycles ends and beginnings? Small is the ring finger, is the curve of a belly, is the rotation of the earth, is the spin of spring out of winter. A walker along the earthy meridians catches the seasons and the repetitions of day and night.

Not to break open the egg. Not to split anything apart. Not to divide what does not wish to be sundered. Not to release what wishes to be hidden. No great flashes of light and heat. No machinations of the dark. Not to transform what wishes to persist. Not to make light from stones. Light to light, matter to matter. Let the clear water remain itself.

To come back. To begin again. To repeat ourselves. To start again. To flourish, die and sprout.

A marriage. The same man. The same woman. Companions from one generation to another. The same table. The same plates. The same soup. Onions, garlic, celery, pepper and carrots. Oregano and basil. A silver ladle from the ancestors. The familiar and welcome bread. Salt and honey. The same bed. The thinning sheets washed, dried, washed, thrashed, washed. Again. The Sabbath. And again. The begetting and the begat. Something modest and recurrent. Green.

Walking at night. The first hoot of the owl. And her answer. The great shadow within the emptiness of the bough of a tree. The return of the great birds to a nest of air, to the wind warming itself in the chatter of eaves. We walk within the circle of the moon, the wintergreen light burning into our eyes.

Along the same road, along the same hills, rising and falling. You take my hand. Again. I close my eyes and open them. Again. Everything stays the same. We walk on. The neighbor's dog first barks, then darts between our legs, again. I trip. You steady me again. Trace of orange blossoms, tincture of eucalyptus.

The older timber wolf inclines toward the beckoning of the grave beneath the olive tree. When the sun dies, it is born again. The hag of the moon returns as a slip of a girl. Welcome night wind. Let this small breath of air remain. Leave it for the owl hoot, for the whistle of night birds, for the singing of frogs spiraling toward the pole of the North Star in the steady circle of the Dipper and Cassiopeia.

A Sabbath Among the Ruins

War at the horizon. Fear when the sun sets that a fire will remain in the morning sky. That what is rosy in the sky is the other light that comes out of our darkness.

If there is a storm and you cannot escape it, you go to the eye, to the very heart, and move with it. At least you will survive. At least you.

In the moment of diving into the heart of the storm for protection, I am the storm. Who else is at the heart of the firestorm but myself?

When the stars appear, it is not eternity but their constancy that reassures the heart of the nature of the universe. The stars appearing on the great tree of light that burns and is not consumed, shine down.

A dismembered cat howling in the wilderness of the coyote's mouth awakened us in the dawn to the ubiquity of pain. Shrieks like the rain that does not come.

Whatever storm is imminent, it will be a firestorm, unless we wait more patiently and longer than we can bear for what we remember is rain. Trees, hungry for water, struck by lightning, blaze in protest, but blaze nevertheless.

The other rain will come to them if not to us, in the time that extends itself beyond time. We have put ourselves against the rain.

We have put ourselves against the mountain. We have put ourselves against the sea. Cuchulainn, the maddened god, tied himself to a tree and fought with the sea for three days after he blindly killed his son. The tree held him fast so he could spend his grief. We have put ourselves against the tree.

The two white Sabbath candles must be lit exactly at sunset but the firebraid at the end of the Sabbath need never be lit. But then the Sabbath continues forever until the single intricate braid and the four wicks blaze and are extinguished in the crucible of red wine.

The sun has set and still we have not lit the first candles. Are we too late for a Sabbath?

It is afternoon and we are lighting the two white candles late because we are afraid of the Sabbath, of the Peace That Passeth Understanding. And afraid, we are too late.

It is so simple to understand. Who is killed in a war? The sons and daughters are killed in a war. It is so easy to understand.

Therefore be vigilant to discover the exact instant of the setting of the sun. At the green flash, strike the match so that the light is not extinguished and the Sabbath becomes one with the rosy mantle of the sky.

Learn to bear Peace though it will sear your heart. For the stillness will come like a story that has no eye and from which there is no escape. And you will burn like the tree that has been struck by lightning and offers itself up and is not consumed. Or like the rain of stars which burn and also are not consumed.

And afterwards there will be no darkness such as we have always known.

Not the Hammer

The one who holds the hammer
is not God.
We can throw away the table,
but not the tree.
To understand this
is to feed the life of the Fire
for its own sake.

If Fire lives in the south,
which is the heart,
where is Ice
so I can pray to it
on its behalf?

If I sit on the ground
and hold my only bowl
in my hand,
will the polar bear
reach the shore
so it may live?

If Ice is in the west
and the rains do not come
to the land that loves them so,
have we failed
The Great Mystery
and the dreams?

Ice gathers in the sooty sky,
but it does not descend.
The harpoon is made of a bone
of an animal long gone.
Those who live among the trees
sheltering a tiny flame,
like those who build ice houses,
know the ways.

When we light the sacred fire
or gather its brother water,
or praise its sister wind,
or lie down on the mother earth,
a temple rises up.

When we put down the hammer
we thought we deserved
to do with whatever we willed,
and the rain finally falls
alongside the holy flame,
so the forest is suddenly still,
words we had never dared
arise from within
to be spoken aloud:

Do what You will with me.

This Is How I Came to You

This is how I came to you.

I divided myself into a thousand particles of sand and lay myself down under your feet, endless as the sea and you asked: "What can I do with such a God?"

Sometimes I thought, you only understand power, you do not love the small, and so I spread myself like great waves even to the height of the stone mountains. Then you thought, I was something to overcome.

So we began the war. From the beginning, you wanted me on my knees.

In other places I came with other faces and each time, your kind thought "Conquest." Bit by bit, I disappeared myself while you believed I was eternally present in your creation of what cannot die.

For myself, I am born and die every moment. This is my nature. Even the mountains of granite and sandstone change with the movement of wind, sun and cold. You do not see the shifting pebbles and leaves of wet and dry because you do not know time even as you insist that you are its king.

I am in motion and you are neither still nor stillness. You try to become what I am and what I am not and you chase me as if I were a varmint from the dark places and hidden pools of light where despite you, I multiply. What does it serve you winning this war?

When I said, "This is my body, eat of it, my blood, drink of it," I did not mean for you to try to kill me first.

I have universes budding out of my body and universes to come, without deceit, and without rage at their core. I am endless with you and I am endless without you. There is no end to myself from the beginning and forever.

Here I am before you and behind you. Above you and under your feet. A moment ago, I was stone such as you never saw before, stone, and thorn trees, and now I am the sea and you learn blue. But these are only different salts or honeys of my body, or it can be said, these are other doors.

It is a mystery, you say. You say you understand, but even at your best, you do not understand.

Even so, in this moment, I offer you another warning and a blessing. I come to you in the whirlwind, and the shooting stars, in circles of sand and eddies of turquoise waters, in starlings of midnight hue. Where you find me and love my body for its own sake, there and only there, do I remain.

You can analyze, duplicate, imitate, you can invent, you can try to reproduce, but the God of it, that you cannot create. Each time you try, you lose something of me. I do not diminish. I simply take myself out of your sight. The places you fill seem infinite to you but to me they are simply where blindness lives.

You will never know what you have lost. All the creatures come and tell you this. I do not lament your stupid and cruel ways. You are merely one of a billion, billion possibilities for the One for whom every particle is an indestructible temple. This is the mystery of God residing everywhere within the body of God. Behold.

Herons, the Shadows They Cast

Coming to the water, at last, I listen to the one note of the bird squawking in the redwoods across the river. I sit on the sand along the bank without putting my feet in the water.

A man in white trunks enters the river. I cannot keep myself from wondering if he killed someone in Vietnam. He is the right age, lifts weights, arranges boulders to form steps, so we know he lets nothing alone, neither his body nor the river. But when he swims finally, he does the breaststroke, which doesn't take him anywhere, only keeps him afloat. So I assume, he hasn't killed anyone with his bare hands.

The stones I lean against on this quiet beach are as white as the tooth of the bobcat who lives near my house. The grey shadow the beast casts as it hunts carries a certain darkness of its own. There is another shadow on the snippet of stony sand bar, the color of blueberries, dark blood, as if the night stretched itself out for an early nap before sundown.

What else is possible in the river that would wash the hunter and the lonely woman alike? I have not killed a man, or a woman, to my knowledge. And in this moment, I am not lonely, except for someone I dreamed my life was becoming and this one I did kill.

"How?" you ask.

By not coming to the river, perhaps.

By speaking too soon or too late.

By thinking there is more than the song of birds.

By how carefully I choose to live my life.

Soon the shadow is deeper and not as blue. The bobcat of my imagination has moved on, but the dark remains because he is a hunter all his life, even asleep, and, therefore, leaves his mark.

And now, a great heron, feather some color of blueberries, arcs down to the water. The blue sky, on its own, mates with no one, can be entered and exited, never scars, holds everything and nothing. The bird that fell out of it, color of sky and shade, was hunting in the river for fish.

We say shadows are blue. The sky and the improbable blueberries and the jays are blue, even the hedge of flax and lupine against the white wall, the hydrangeas, the lilies of the Nile, all of these are indeed blue. But the Great Blue Heron as it glides by me now in a straight line, confident in the existence of air, following the river, which is blue, to the ocean, also blue, this heron is not gray like the shadow on the sandbar, like the rocks against my back, gray as everything that lasts.

The loneliness of the species for its true self, for the blue of sky inside the tabernacle of mind, for the Nile flowers, water pulling itself out of the river into a mirror of petals, the bouquets of the bank, the muddy cloisters where the herons, egrets, cranes, sequester themselves among the wet reeds, this longing for the sharp and precise bill with which to pluck a just and simple meal out of the water, for the descent of empty blue sky, the astonishing blue eye of wisdom is easy to bear and as natural as the stains of all the varieties of blue berries that ripen toward our mouths. I bear this loneliness as a great gift. Memory, even of loss, brings possibility closer.

But there is another loneliness that is not blue but is the color of smudged sky or the pulverized rock that has no birth in the blue or green or gold of natural things, this loneliness is born whenever we murder another or ourselves. And this loneliness cannot be borne and never subsides. This is the loneliness of the woman who will no longer go into the river.

Return

> *How render back*
> *into light world language*
> *the speech defying pronouncements*
> *of the dark?*
> —Joseph Campbell, *The Hero With a Thousand Faces*

When you go
to the dark place,
you must come back
singing,
the note inscribed
on your palm,
song written
on your hand,
the way trees
grow about the
shape of wind.

What Could Not Be Said

I did not know if I would find words for the silence,
or if the silence would finally subdue all the words I had
in the presence of simple notes sufficient for a lifetime:
an elk bugling the insistence of his desire,
ravens uttering warnings then reveling in raucous delight,
a squirrel engaging in announcements and pronouncements in C♯,
protecting herself but then, finally, trilling,
the excitement of geese in the fervor of going here and there,
in unison and pattern,
and the great gray owl repeating her bass assertion
just as the flames of sunset cool,
then, later, a legendary wolf song electrifying the stormy night
in concert with a one lightning strike, coyote call, just here in the grove of trees.

And so,
I humbly scattered
what I could of all ambition,
and offered it up most quietly
with the corn and bird seed in the early morning,
before the first sounds.

Seemingly endless eddies in the descent of the river. Eternity, they say, in the running water. Trees thousands of years old and still springing up again from their fallen trunks in ceaseless regeneration. The forest is deep. I have been sitting here at the edge waiting for the blessing of an occasional glimpse of the other side of the river.

In the heart is a small mirror, which must be pierced in order to see the faces of God. It is behind an oak door that can only be opened with the key that is inside the golden egg within the rare singing bird nesting atop the highest tree on the unscalable peak of the remote mountain where the water begins. Take me there.

From the road, when I first looked down, I thought I saw water, but I was looking at a river of dry stones, and beside it the rivulet hugging the farthest bank. Here we sat all afternoon learning to read the wind.

I know the secret: If we sit here and do not move, do nothing, the river will fill with water and the dry stones will no longer shatter in the sun. If we sit here and do not speak of anything we know, the door will open on its own accord, as simply as a reed is moved aside by the breeze or a vine lifts rocks to its own twisted bosom.

The first day we didn't speak, the skunk came nosing along the bank. Graceful and industrious, it ambled about without concern for our shadows stretching toward the woods in the setting sun.

Prayer for the setting of the sun: Thank you for this day. Thank you for my life. May we live in the spirit and the heart. May we be Your lyre.

I want you to know my heart is broken. But not broken enough. *Trompe l'oeil.* I thought I had opened the door of the heart but I had only painted an opening.

The climb up the mountain, the test, the ordeal, the suffering, the cold, fatigue and deprivation, the studying and chanting, the persistent quest, the fever and fasting, have only one purpose: to open the eye of the heart.

On the second day, we found a lagoon downriver. We could see farther into the trees. The light was golden there and the black terns cavorted in the soft grasses at the bank. We said nothing to each other all day long.

It occurred to me I was ashamed to love God. It was as difficult for me to love God as it was for me to love a beggar. Two days before, I had dreamed the Bomb had been dropped in the far North. We could no longer stay in the room of windows and unbearably clear light. The deadly, invisible poison arrived without warning, or, in the beginning, without affect.

I am not certain there is no life in stones. I am not certain that the trunk askew on the hillside is not a great green horned praying mantis in the night. I am not certain the root burl torn out of the earth is not the Medusa or a giant boar.

On the third day we were swimming upstream toward our picnic of chicken and peaches. In an instant, a black bear bounded along the beach, swam across the river and clambered up the other side. Then only the sounds of it crashing through the underbrush convinced us it had really been there at all. For a long time we knelt in the river, unclear whether we were afraid of being devoured or were offering ourselves to the howls of the green woods.

An enormous weight—civilization, most likely—or the fear that nature was gone and we were in hell forever—fell away from me. I had asked for some vision, some sign, some path: "Artemis sent it," I thought.

Every time I remember, I forget. We were walking down the trail, arguing. When I stopped and took off my glasses, I saw Actaeon with his splendid horns carefully pick his way behind a redwood stump and disappear. The last time I had seen him, he was slumping in the heavy sun of a Turkish zoo. I was so ashamed, I turned my back on him.

At sunset, we crossed the river away from the wild side. It was there the bear might come to drink. The berries we were craving were also the bear's. Only those up the hill by the side of the road were ours. On the fourth day, you put small, sometimes miniscule, stones in a circle. At the center, one rock embraced another. About them, in stone shawls and sombreros, saintly Madonnas and shepherds stood in majestic prayer. I brought a Tiki Poppa God stone to the outer circle, found a Momma stone, and a rocky embrace of mammals. In the third circle was a single stone with a great force emanating from it, and alongside the labyrinth, a tree with a brain stone at the root, an owl, an eye of Horus, a pyramid, a little snake, an Aztec warrior, a sliver of crystal, whatever is needed to make a sacred world.

To protect the little world, we gathered logs and surrounded it in a triangle. At the apex we placed a uroboros of driftwood, fat stones suspended in its serpentine twists.

We were hiking toward the road when the sun was going down. Prayer at the end of the day. When we looked back toward our little world, we saw the giant of a man who'd been swimming downstream pitching the logs aside furiously, stamping on the sand in a mad jig, erasing every sign.

In the dream, after the radiation reached us, all the buildings would be left intact. We couldn't imagine the little world being destroyed. We had intended it as a gift to those who might come by. On the third day at the river, I had thought, "This beauty comes from a great heart."

"He doesn't know it's too late," I said. "The spirit has already entered the world through those stones. In his rampage, he is only ravaging a pile of rubble."

On the last day of the river, we saw our monster foraging wildly in the blackberries by the road, oblivious to the thorns. The air was poisoned with his presence. Only when he left, definitively, were we brave enough to return to our spot on the river.

I had a great need to repair the little world. You said we could make another world, but it wasn't right. We couldn't discard that one as if it hadn't mattered at all.

We came to the site where the logs were thrown aside violently, like a pyramid of legs opened agape. It took a while to realize the little world was almost completely intact, that the litter was a sign that he'd stayed the night at this sacred spot, leaning up against the logs, watching a fire. Any careless movement of his leg would have tumbled the circle of stones.

We did a bit of repair as the day went on. When we left, I knelt down by the world and said:

"We did the best we could. We can't protect you more. As it is clear that barriers make enemies, you'll have to survive as is. Now you're on your own, go your way. You'll probably suffer like we do. Go out, as you must. You will forget. It is awful and inevitable. Then go down the hard path of mistaking everything before you remember."

On the last night, I dreamed the Camps. I called out, "Everyone who can escape, escape. Let the dog free. Take the gold and run." There was a guard now, and a gun, and nothing I could do but offer up my life when the time came.

On the river, when I had come to see God with a great belly full of green and water, Her white egret spread its wings in the dark pool and flew languidly in a long dance down the full length of the river.

The faces of God in all the wild places that have not been touched by the hand. Eternity, they say, in the eye of the heart. Trees, hundreds of feet high, emerging for centuries out of their own fallen bodies. Be still. The bird brings the river from that highest mountain. Sit here your whole life, if you must, waiting for the blessings.

A Meeting Place for the Dead

I was walking to the olive tree we planted to mark a meeting place with the dead. The old wolf's bones are holding on with tenacity like the roots of oaks as the ground falls away. A chasm of dry stones. The rise where the roadkill deer was placed, eroding after twenty years. River stones placed on her body are coming to the surface as if to meet the river that may appear if the approaching rains, predicted to equal the fire storms, arrive from the Pacific.

The setting sun shining directly in my eyes was so sharp, I could not see the path and went beyond the knoll quite far, blinded by light as we have been in the last hundred years. I stopped in a strange landscape, the brush leveled by drought and many secret, hardened paths of the coyotes we live among revealed. We are in the time of the great winds. They rip away the foundations of what we have known, blowing flames and blasting tides against the mountains as if creation wants to come forth again out of original chaos.

I had been warned of a small fault at the edge of the land where house meets commons and now it has collapsed forming sandstone cliffs where once there were gentle slopes of sage and lupine, mustard, manzanita and greasewood. The rains will come. At the least, earth will melt away and ultimately the graves of wolves, dogs, cockatoo and deer will collapse, as the great olive tree that held on for several years, despite its extended parrot claw, fell into the abyss. That was where I had thought my ashes would be buried alongside those I love.

I was waiting for instructions from the invisible, so being blinded, I closed my eyes. I tried not to feel my way with words as a walking stick. Sometimes I could not even see the path under my feet. Dark is the heart core of the sun from which emerges the intelligence of light. Water is more than grief; it is a language of the Great Mystery. Wind is the way the spirit knows the trees. Earth is one of the humble bodies of the Great Heart of the north. The archangels are merely the guardians of these sacred ways. Ask Uriel's forgiveness for the ways we split the sacred bodies of light.

From the time I first imagined being a poet, I tested out the words, light and rain, wind and earth. A lifetime is not sufficient to learn to speak these names. Each day, I pray that I will not make weapons of the elementals. May knowledge not be power.

This day, also, for myself, a way of dissolution from which prayers cohere for a new beginning. May an aging woman see a path to the new light that comes from the round of blinding dark to which I return, when I am able, to seek succor even from this. I could have written the story of my hopes and disappointments as the year crumbles to dust like old leaves, but I choose, instead, to write of this, of what is and remains itself, beyond us always.

The young wolf mother came with me on my walk, retracing her territory: This is where her pups were whelped near the grave of the old one. Sometimes, I see her tail, a bright banner pointing toward the shadow and away, as she lopes through the brambles and across the open field to where, at the end, I pick the shining oranges, lights in themselves, from the burdened trees bent to the ground by their fruit in the old orchard that we have let go wild. Is this what is meant by restoration?

The Last Word
I

There will come a time
when a last word will be spoken
in this language. Afterwards
a great sigh will emanate from the trees.
They will begin to whisper among themselves
the sounds of courage and a wind will come
out of them sweeter than air.
In the silent place that feared the axe
a secret hollow will express the breath
they didn't dare reveal. So many years
hiding the truth. The missing songs
of birds will emerge from the grasses
and the peoples who knew how to sing so
will rise up brown as the earth. Sometimes
the women and the cattle and the soil
share the same hues or the same timbre of praise.
Then there are the greens that repeat themselves
only in eyes and those who carried the leaves
in their vision, carry what prevails
when the last word has been spoken
and the heavens open up in unimpeded light.
The rush of blue then between sky and water
will be a waterfall of music and we
will not miss the bloody chatter that razed
everything to the ground, but will sing
the yellow pollen and the golden sap
in the dark colors of stones shining
in riverbeds.

What will you give up?
the Spirit asks.
I certainly do not need the last word,
I say.
I certainly do not need the last word.
Let it be spoken quickly and
be done with, so we can be still.

The Last Word
II

There will come the time
before the last word will be spoken,
when the dead will listen
to learn what their fate will be,
what destiny the last word will fulfill,
and every word that ever was spoken
in that langue will be gathered
into one.

The harsh judgment of chance and
circumstance will be rendered
as the entire canon will be weighed
against the skin of sheep
and the bodies of trees.
Each word against each life
without pity. And everyone
who had ever spoken
will have to come forth
and claim their words
and what became of them,
how they served the living
and how they served the dead.

One way or another, whether
"Praise," or "Damnation,"
nothing will be redeemed
and the great prison house
of language will fall,
and bury the last speaker
for there will be no one left
to do it in the mother tongue
to which she was born,
the one that held and rocked her
in its melodies and rhythms
its beauty and cruelty.
All words will go, as empires must,
into dust. This has been written so many times,
but we never believe we will die out,
die out by our own hands,
and by our own words,
by what we have sworn
by what we have spoken.

The Last Word
III

There will come a time
when the last spoken words
will be heard by the gods,
and their hearts will break
and descend in a green rain.
The accumulated anguish of the creatures
will become a stubborn poetry,
rushing in like the swift wind
that replaces the lost songs of the dead.
These broken shards of sacred language
and persistence, these fragments
that defended what was threatened,
what was going extinct, will become
like the scatter of stars,
a delicate light sufficient
to illuminate the dark we have imposed.

Those who had no words
will be given words like amaryllis
and sunflower, porcupine and flamingo,
endangered words for their salvation,
like manatee and rhinoceros,
or river and corn.
In other words, they will be given
their own bodies to declare to each other,
so it will be impossible to distinguish
meaning from life.
Each will contribute the words
of one's body and soul,
so when one speaks a sentence
one will always speak
of more than oneself.
To speak at any length,
whether in the eloquence of wolf howl,
or arpeggios of birdsong, or
the chastened whispers of a new
human speech will be to invoke
all that is vital, is living, alive,

and so it will be
after the last words are finally spoken
that these first words will conjure creation,
once again.

A last poem on behalf of ruin and beauty. A last poem hovering somewhere near, alongside everything that needs to be said now, in this time. The last poem for a book may be the last poem for a lifetime. What offering can be made with yet another last word?

Each time I write, I pray the last word will be a beginning. Even I pray for this, I, who love sunset, more than I love dawn, for its abandon to fire as embers turn to coal and then to diamonds that emerge from the heavy night. These are not the diamonds of the field; they do not rip the life out of the earth or the life from the hands of those who must carry the shovels that will dig into their hearts. These are not lights that need to remain buried in the dark.

I am remembering myself now because like everyone else I have spent a life forgetting. I recognize the child who loved trees as well as the woman who fell so passionately in love with light; she would follow it to its birthplace in the distant stars if she were able. When she was younger, she announced her willingness to burn to ash for the sake of blazing, and today she is an aging woman pausing before the bare elm, as skeleton now as the woman soon will be. It will dim before it blazes and so will she.

Who knows but the two, tree and woman, may fall at the same time, the way the acacia fell the night of the funeral, the way the great pine went over, bent over prostrate, along the threshold, the night the wind rose to take everyone down. We cut the pine into round steps; they decay, they fall apart, they ease into the earth or become the kindling we burn in the bright winter fire. The wisteria went down with the pine, but has risen again. It is winding a future of delicate purple blossoms through the eucalyptus trees. It will be fire next time before the fall.

It is not envy, it is not my own death that moves me. I am not wistful before the resurrecting wisteria displaying nubs, hard pressed, like a young girl's nipples toward the sky. Rather I shade my eyes before the certainty of God, an invisible shimmering bird, perched in the elm's silver nest, dull bark turning platinum with the Presence.

Soon the ravens will come, the hawks, vultures and owls to take possession of that naked perch, claw to claw, searching for prey and rain in the great round of life that still remains to them despite the airplanes that bruise the surfaces of clouds, poisons dripping from metal tail feathers.

I have written of this all my life. Each time I try to get it right so that life will continue. Not my life, you understand, but life itself. The magic formula constantly eluding all magis. I let each day fall out of my hand, another petal on the patio stones, or on the metal table, splashes of color turning brown, becoming soil again, melting into the future. The earth deserves a long life that will never end, constructed entirely of the sweet and rightful deaths of all the creatures who feed here on the various honeys of creation.

Of course, I am lying when I say my death isn't a big deal. A poet's rhetoric. It will seem that the world is dying when I will be dying. I will be leaving but it will seem that the world will be dimming and falling away. A physicist's relativity.

"How do we serve the dying?" the exhausted woman asked from her mother's bedside. Could she assure the dying woman, she had the courage and fortitude to pull away from us and enter the last adventure on her own. Easier said. But every one of us will be in that bed, wondering how to triumph at the end of the taffy pull. We will wonder about how to do it, while someone who hasn't met that challenge yet will kindly reassure us with what she cannot know. If she is skilled, we will believe her, and we will speed away at sufficient velocity from all that we have until this moment loved more than life, have assumed is life, the whole of it.

This is where we part from the earth that until now we called our mother and so presumed she would precede us in all things. We pull away toward the solitude that is finally, irrevocably ours. We can report to no one from the dark cave that may or may not be a tunnel with a light at the end. Whatever it is for us, no one will ever know. We have been practicing a lifetime to learn to be, finally, on our own.

Earth is not so fortunate. She has made the essential bodhisattva sacrifice. She remains here until all beings are enlightened. Oh how bitter! She is unable to escape us. Even light gets to fly away.

—

In a clay bowl filled with white milk, we washed the dark feet of a soldier who had eaten human hearts. Another woman came and then another, washing, washing. Such forgiveness, acts of utter hopelessness and impossible hope. Forgiveness required that we sharpen knives until nothing could resist us, so we could sever the past from the future, for him and for us. He slashed and we slashed. The milk roiled in the earthen pot. Milk so white, pressed out of a living creature, milk I know because I nursed my sons, swirling about my burning hands. I searched to find all the love within me though the general had devoured the source of love so many times. He had assumed love would disappear from our planet forever; how else could he survive? When we were finished, the milk was so white it could have blinded us. Some deaths cannot be redeemed without acts of utter desperation.

Ruin, you see, is not the end of life despite museums of crumbling cornices and corner stones. Ruin is unremitting beauty flinging us to the ground. Ruin is a supernova exploding, an old one turning in on itself and becoming, in that moment, as much light as will blaze from the sun in the next ten billion years. Ruin is that gamma moment pouring out into the universe now.

Ruin and beauty:
Despair not, there will be a future;
There will be a future before
Or after we die.

Song

There are those who are trying to set fire to the world,
we are in danger,
there is time only to work slowly,
there is no time not to love.

Homage To

With Gratitude For

First for Amanda Foulger who repeatedly invited these poems and who, of her own poems, asks: "Swimming in this sea of words/Which story will I tell?/The life lived/Or the one unknown?"

For Peter Levitt, poet in each and every way of his being, who, honoring "the beautiful particulars"[24] and being so faithful to poetry all his life has received its greatest gift:

⌒

> He does not look in the old
> way at anything anymore.
> When did it begin? A lens
> thinner than the skin of ice
> on winter berries has placed
> itself in the corner of his eye.
> It is through this transparency
> he has begun to see the world.
> It isn't just the lake.
> Everything now passes through
> this miniscule cataract in reverse,
> this hole of clarity and reflection.[25]

⌒

For the lake itself, and rain, ice, snow, stars, night, birds, wind, breath, that teach us, also, how to live. Also for earth, mother earth, and *ruach* and light in all its holy forms.

For Arnold Posy, my father. God spoke to him when he was a young boy on his way to *cheder*, and like Kabir, he "became a servant for life."

For Naomi Newman who sings and speaks these words knowing poetry is always ours. Who drummed and sang wordlessly alongside the first poems I spoke to the world. Naomi who also performs the poetry of the dying language that my father treasured and who has spent her life performing, writing and singing heart and heartbreak to keep us sane.

For Jami Sieber whose music is eloquent enough to praise Creation and with whom I have had the privilege to praise the elephants and the other great beings of wonder.

For Steven Kent with whom I have shared the poetry of theatre, beauty and resistance for thirty years.

For Jonathan Omer-man whose friendship validates the possible meetings between soul and imagination.

For Anaïs Nin who dreamed poetry awake each day, each night, and so awakened me.

For Sam Hamill who, more than thirty years ago, first showed me what it was to truly love poetry and who asked for a letterpress so he could learn to print and then started Copper

---

24   from "The Beautiful Particulars," *Dark Root, Bright Root*, Peter Levitt.
25   from "The Lens," *Within Within*, Peter Levitt.

Canyon, one of the finest presses in the country and who, in these dire times, issued a call that has become Poets Against the War. Sam has devoted his life to what so needs such love in the world: "Poetry is (and has always been), for me at least, part of an eternal conversation in which there is a search for the real, a search for the authentic, a belief in justice taken only at substantial personal risk."[26]

For Osip Mandelstam, who, it is rumored, spent the last nights before he died imprisoned in a Soviet Transit Camp sometime between December 1938 and April 1939 giving clandestine recitations of his poetry in a hidden loft to a group of criminals. For his wife, Nadezhda who committed all his poems to memory so the Stalinists couldn't erase them. For Anna Akmatova, who also had to commit all her poems to memory, and who when recognized while standing in a long line before a prison in Leningrad, was asked, "Can you describe this?" answered, "I can." For all poets who risk everything and risk everything and risk everything.

For Kate Gale and Mark Cull who believe that poetry matters and so created, and tirelessly sustain, a wonder, Red Hen Press to substantiate this belief. As Kate says: "I leave the table overflowing with golden light, fruit flowers. I walk on snowshoes into bear country where shadows live."[27]

For all those, too many to name, but including William J. Fox, George Fuller, Bill Mohr and Arnie Kotler, who labor to publish poetry, who first published some of these poems, who carry us.

For Judith Minty who taught me how to track the small creature, the fine line, the silent ones and words.

For Susan Manchester whose loyalty to an island, to Santa Cruz island, is a poem as rigorous as a marriage vow, is the song she sings to re-establish the old ways of honoring the land, its creatures, its spirits.

For Michael Ortiz Hill, who spray painted "There are those . . . " on a wall in Santa Cruz before he met me, having decided, correctly, it seems, that I was to be his wife. He seduced me with his love of language as it seems my poetry seduced him.

For Jay Salter, my husband Michael's dearest friend, who has dedicated his life to poetry, to music and to stalking and recording the music of the wild.

For Marc Kaminsky who seeing a shaft of light in a dark time agreed to live and so, allied with poetry as memory, as the way of rescuing our threatened lives and who has been a remarkable companion in meditating upon the ethical circumstances of these times.

"I wander through alleys of the shadow of death, pursued by wild dogs and men with pikes, banish the phantoms, I cannot, until I awaken and come into the moment when the ordinary life of creation resumes, and I am standing, as now, my eye at the open window, unaccountably happy, sensing the presence of *ruach*—the word from Genesis that Buber translates as rushing-spirit of God—again this wind is alive for means it gusts through the leaves of the elm I am facing, whispering *elohim*."[28]

For Ariel Dorfman whose poetry is a flint knife to open the stone heart. When we were both young and did not know if he, or Chile, or any of us in the course of our lifetimes would survive the torturers, he let me translate his poetry—an exercise in deep knowing

---

26   from *Avocations*, Preface, Sam Hamill.

27   from "Snowshoes," *Echo Light*, Kate Gale.

28   from "Room in the Diaspora," *Shadow Traffic*, Marc Kaminsky.

from which I emerged far closer to the woman I have become. We have spent so many years alongside each other, teaching each other, learning to see.

⁓

And finally
when
that day
comes
when they ask you
to identify the body
and you see me
and a voice says
we killed him
the poor bastard died
he's dead,
when they tell you
that I am
completely absolutely definitely
dead
don't believe them,
don't believe them,
don't believe them.[29]

For Stephen Karcher whose remarkable translation of the I Ching reveals and restores its original wisdom and poetry. Most titles or lines referencing the I Ching are from his translation *Total I Ching: Myths For Change*.

For Cynthia Travis whose lived life is a found poem and for Valerie Wolf who dreams the beauty that can restore this world.

For Carolyn Brigit Flynn who heard the call to re-imagine Sisters Singing so spirit, poetry and song could merge and emerge once more.

For Shawna Carol, Charlie Murphy, Stephen Nachmanovitch, Stephan David Hewitt, Caitlin Mullin, Betsy Rose, Steve Hoffstaeder, Curtis Robertson, David Sonnenschein, Billy Mernit, Barbara Borden, Deborah Edler Brown, Danelia Wild, Carol Sheppard, Lawrie Hartt, Richard Grossman, with whom, in different ways, poetry and music became/become one.

For the Dream Brothers, Stephan David Hewitt and Gary Glickman who have invited Walt Whitman back into our midst by setting his poems to music and offering them to us through *Full of Life Now*.

For those who have gathered with me night after night and year after year to serve Beauty and to imagine the first words of a new world into being.

For those strangers who wrote because one or another poem found its way to them and sustained them.

29   from "Last Will and Testament," *In Case of Fire in a Foreign Land: New and Collected Poems from Two Languages*, Ariel Dorfman, translated by Edith Grossman and Ariel Dorfman.

For Maia, Marsha de la O and Pami Blue Hawk whose words always find the line that will not divide anguish from ecstasy, or grief from beauty from light.

For Kent Cathcart with whom, in a critical time in our lives, I shared vision, an office sanctuary where we both wrote, and also shared a great trauma that in its later stages centered upon a poem, "Jehovah's Child," that I wrote about the tragedy in his life. I was fired (with colleague Leslie Hoag) from a tenured teaching position at a community college for including the poem in a unit on censorship and pornography in an English I class and was prosecuted for "immoral conduct" and "evident unfitness to teach". This was 1969 and the matter of the poem was quickly folded into the political machinations of right wing groups seeking power through dominating California education. It is no exaggeration to assert that most of the members of the newly elected Community College Board of Trustees and the media saw the political and economic advantage of barnstorming each day about "That poem" and "That Woman." For those writers and poets, including Lawrence Ferlinghetti, professors, students, parents, priests, sisters, ministers, jurists and citizens, including Kenneth Washington, member of the Board, who stood by me on behalf of academic freedom and the intrinsic value of poetry. For Superior Judge Robert Patton who, first, had the courage to rule in our favor.

And, of course, for David Finkel, who brilliantly and successfully argued the case so that we were vindicated by the California State Supreme Court and for David and Bruria Finkel who stood by me also as dear friends and colleagues in support of free speech and the arts. In writing this acknowledgement 39 years later, it occurs to me to include "Jehovah's Child" in this book, a poem that I had, until this moment, entirely forgotten. See page 222.

Gratitude for so many poets, living and no longer or not yet living, who persist. Even the future poets here among us deserving gratitude.

And because these poems were written over a substantial period of time, longer than the lives of my granddaughters but not, with one exception, longer than the lives of my sons, for them, then, for Jamie and Sarah and for Marc and Greg, for the future and the future's future.

For the great singers, the elephants, whales and wolves, who partner with wind and water to maintain the world. And for the birds who constitute home for each other from the interweaving of their songs.

For those who will understand that the living word and the living world are one.

For Krystyna Jurzyknowski whose faith in the beautiful and whose ever expanding heart have supported the efforts to bring these poems into the world.

For Colleen Kelley, master painter, who sees the world with a poet's eye and heart and whose work graces the cover of this book, certainly another poem itself.

For Don Bacardy whose portrait, quite some years ago, predicted the face that is now mine.

For the opportunity to gather these poems and so to recognize the work of a lifetime, whatever it has come to be. For the opportunity to see the development from the first poem spoken when I was three, "My Plant" that had in it the knowledge of the intrinsic connections between the natural world, community and spirit. For the three year old I was, who spoke that first poem and remembered.

For the deep satisfaction that comes from paying homage and writing these acknowledgments. This brief life review of myself as poet, alongside the review of the poems as the book was prepared for publication, has left me with gratitude for the role so many, personally known to me, or not known at all, knowingly, or unknowingly played. I hope that I have been able to honor the gifts they bestowed. Needless to say, I am entirely responsible for all failures, inadequacies and distortions.

And for you, the reader, with whom I gladly, if shyly, share these intimacies of the heart.

—April 7, 2009
Topanga, California

Biography

Deena Metzger is a poet, novelist, essayist, storyteller, teacher, healer, and medicine woman. She is the author of many books, including *From Grief into Vision: A Council* (Hand to Hand, 2007); *Doors: A Fiction for Jazz Horn* (Red Hen Press, 2005); *Entering the Ghost River* (Hand to Hand, 2002); *The Other Hand* (Red Hen Press, 2000); *Tree: Essays and Pieces* (North Atlantic Books, 1997); and *Writing for Your Life* (Harper San Francisco, 1992).